SILLY WOMAN THAT AIN'T YOUR HUSBAND

THERESA HORNES

Theresa Hornes

Silly Woman That Ain't Your Husband

ISBN: 978-0-557-84860-7

Contact Information:
theresahornes@yahoo.com
courageunderfire8@yahoo.com
www.sillywomanthataintyourhusband.webs.com/

Dedications

Lord, thank you for showing me all things are possible to them that believe. I did not think a book was in my future. Moreover, when you gave me the title I did not think I would ever finish this book. Yet, you knew it was possible. I love you and praise you for bringing out the best in me!

Shawntise, I thank you for giving me your ear when I needed it. You helped me more than you know.

Justin, you came home one afternoon and told me your friend asked what your mother did for a living. You told him I was a writer and that I was working on my book. My heart was truly touched.

My sincere thanks go to **Pastor Tonia Brown** and **Angelica Dodson** for pushing me to finish this book.

I want to thank **Dionne Beynum** for her honesty, laughter and straight talk.

Special thanks go to my husband **Gerald** for his love and support. Thank you for being a sounding board even during your Redskin games! Your prayers made all the difference.

Foreword

It is my honor to write the foreword for this book. It is a book for this time. I say this not because the author is my wife and an anointed woman of God but because in today's society we have too many woman of God falling into traps set by the enemy. They are dating and marrying the wrong men, an assignment sent by Satan himself. This is all in an effort to hinder and/or stop their ministry from going forth. I have seen my wife cry out to the Lord on behalf of women who have forsaken God, their children and their futures to be with a man God has not ordained for their lives. She desires total restoration for the women of God and for them to live a lifestyle that is pleasing to the Father.

I found a "good thing" when I found Theresa and have received favor from the Lord. She is holding to the standard of holiness when others seem to be slowly letting go and accepting anything as right. I praise God for giving her to me and I am thankful to God for the anointing upon her life. I know that through you reading the book the anointing upon her will be a blessing to you as well.

Take heed to yourselves, that your heart be not deceived, and ye turn aside, and serve other gods, and worship them; And then the LORD's wrath be kindled against you, and he shut up the heaven, that there be no rain, and that the land yield not her fruit; and lest ye perish quickly from off the good land which the LORD giveth you. Deuteronomy 11:16 KJV

Pastor Gerald Hornes

Introduction

While writing this book I faced many struggles. God wanted me to share stories from my life and the lives of other women that were deeply personal and downright painful. I put the pen down so many times out of frustration and He would always give me a reason to pick the pen back up and write. After the last occurrence of putting my pen down, my daughter and I took a bus ride. We greeted this older woman as she came onto the bus. She sat down behind me and told us how refreshing it was to see young women be cordial. She complimented us on our appearance and the manner in which we behaved. She went on to share her view about the women of today. How they were wasting their lives on no good men.

A woman sitting across from us interjected and said, "I got rid of my no good man." We all smiled. She further went on to say that, she has a new man who treats her good. She explained his goodness to us as we rode along. The older woman told her to be careful because those types can be tricksters as well. Then she blurted out that her husband had chopped her in the head with an axe back in 1979. We all gasped when we heard this. She said he did this because she had questioned him about where the rest of his paycheck was after he gave her only fifteen dollars. She narrowly escaped with her life! Upon her release from the hospital, she never went back to him. She asked us the question, "What sense does it make to go back to a man that tried to kill you?"

The older woman went on to share that years later he lay dying in the same hospital where he had put her years earlier. He sent messages by their children requesting to see her. She told them no on several occasions but after much prodding; they convinced her to go see him. When she arrived, all he wanted to know was if he could come home with her to die. She told him no. She was not having any of that! Before my daughter and I exited the bus, I looked at her and said, "It was God's grace and mercy that keep you."

She agreed whole-heartedly. After meeting this woman and hearing her story, I knew I had to obey God and publish this book.

God is calling His daughters out of ungodly relationships. These types of relationships are never pleasing to God nor is there any benefit to you. God sent me to tell you "Enough is enough!" He is tired of his daughters having itching ears. Stop believing false prophecies that so and so is your husband. Do not believe every spirit that is talking to you. God taught me this lesson first hand.

While a babe in Christ I attended a church service where I heard a spirit say to me, "He is your husband." The "he" that spirit was talking about was the pastor of the church. This pastor was single and had been for years. Most of the women in that church already thought he was their husband. The women in the church thought that he was their husband as well. I heard the voice of the Lord say to me, "Rebuke that spirit in the name of Jesus." "Shake it off of you and command it to leave the service." I did exactly as God said. I literally saw the spirit run out of the church! Before this point, I had never thought about this man in that way. I did not find him attractive nor was he my type. I thank God for the Holy Spirit, having an ear to hear the voice of truth and obeying. After that incident, I refused to go back to that church and I learned a very valuable lesson. Every thought that comes to your mind is not always your own! There are still women to this day who are attending this church and still believe they are going to be his wife.

For a time is coming when people will no longer listen to sound and wholesome teaching. They will follow their own desires and will look for teachers who will tell them whatever their itching ears want to hear. They will reject the truth and chase after myths. 2 Timothy 4:3-4 AMP

God is not going to send you on some wild goose chase after a man that is not your husband. He is able to speak to a man concerning you being his wife. He does not need your help. Besides, it is not in our makeup to chase after a man but our desperation makes us do so! This type of thing happens because we tend to read more into a situation than it really is. Let me explain. If this man has not spoken to you beyond small talk after a few months, do not assume that he wants you or that you are the one. Just because he smiled at you and exchanged polite conversation does not mean he want you for a wife. Men know exactly what they want and whom they want to marry! If you are the one, he will not let you get away. If your man has not asked you to marry him after a year, you need to move on. Why waste two or more years of your life waiting on him to decide if you are worth marrying or not. If he has asked you to marry him with a ring as proof and a date has not been set after a few months you need to give back the ring and move on. More than likely, the ring was given so that you would stop nagging him about marrying you. You are wasting your time waiting for him to decide on a wedding date. Come out of the delusion (a fixed belief that is false, fanciful, or derived from deception). Get yourself together. Stop fornicating! Stop cohabitating! Move on!

Recently after prayer, the Lord laid one of my sister's on my heart and pointed out that she has been in a relationship with her boyfriend for almost **thirty years!** The very thought of this weighed heavy on my heart but it is a terrible reminder of how easy it is for any of us to end up in this same situation when we don't obey God. This man never brought anything positive to her life! He sowed nothing of value into the lives of her children. From where they lived to what car they drove, it all belonged to her. Just a few years ago, God in His loving kindness was trying to give her a new lease on life and she chose her life with this man over what the Father wanted to do for her. She has wasted so much precious time on a man that was not and is not the will of God for her life. The devastating part is that the only thing she has to show for her near thirty-year investment is a mean, sick, alcoholic who verbally abuses her and her immediate family without shame. This is not what our loving Father intended for his daughters.

God's prophet Juanita Bynum warned us years ago with "No More Sheets." We obeyed for a while, and then we turned back to our wicked ways and committed adultery against God. Now God is warning us again to come out of sexual sin and ungodly relationships. He wants us to be holy as He is holy. We are not to be as the foolish virgins who wasted their oil and when Jesus arrived; they did not have enough oil to get them to the wedding feast. The Lord mean serious business and I must sound the alarm once again.

After seven days the LORD gave me a message. He said, "Son of man, I have appointed you as a watchman for Israel. Whenever you receive a message from me, warn people immediately. If I warn the wicked, saying, 'You are under the penalty of death,' but you fail to deliver the warning, they will die in their sins. And I will hold you responsible for their deaths. If you warn them and they refuse to repent and keep on sinning, they will die in their sins. But you will have saved yourself because you obeyed me.

"If righteous people turn away from their righteous behavior and ignore the obstacles I put in their way, they will die. And if you do not warn them, they will die in their sins. None of their righteous acts will be remembered, and I will hold you responsible for their deaths. But if you warn righteous people not to sin and they listen to you and do not sin, they will live, and you will have saved yourself, too." Ezekiel 3:16-21 NLT

God is commanding you to be holy. I pray you will take heed and obey the voice of the Lord!

Table of Contents

PART 1

YOU

Chapter 1

SILLY WOMAN DEFINED

While I was on my way to work one morning the Lord spoke to me and said, "Silly Woman That Ain't Your Husband." I responded, "Lord what are you are talking about?" He said, "This is the title of your book. This is what my daughters have become. It grieves me to hear their prayers full of pain and sorrow. Their heartache could be avoided if they obey my word." The Holy Spirit began to bring to my memory what I went through with men and the experiences of other women whom I knew. God does not like His daughters taken advantage of and He wants you to be tired of it too.

The word silly is defined as weak-minded or lacking good sense, stupid or foolish.

But mark this: There will be terrible times in the last days. People will be lovers of themselves, lovers of money, boastful, proud, abusive, disobedient to their parents, ungrateful, unholy, without love, unforgiving, slanderous, without self-control, brutal, not lovers of the good, treacherous, rash, conceited, lovers of pleasure rather than lovers of God—having a form of godliness but denying its power. Have nothing to do with them.

They are the kind who worm their way into homes and gain control over weak-willed [silly] women, who are loaded down with sins and are swayed by all kinds of evil desires, always learning but never able to acknowledge the truth. 2 Timothy 3:1-7 NIV

Do you remember Sampson? God chose him before birth to fight and destroy the Philistine army. He does a good job at first then he lets his desire for foreign women pull him away. His mother and father warned him not to mess with those women. They even ask him what is wrong with the Hebrew women God chose for him. He tells them they have no flavor. He likes them exotic and erotic. Despite his parents protest he goes and hooks up with a Philistine woman named Delilah. This woman has all the right moves and she knows all the tricks. Delilah blows Sampson's mind! Now he is lying in her bed acting all silly. Every time she thought, he had revealed the source of his strength her mob would come in to kill him. Each time Sampson fought them off. Delilah knew he was holding back on her so she used tears and cunning words to seduce him. She wants to know the secret of his strength that her people may destroy him. He has been a thorn in their side for years! Delilah's mission is to get the job done and she is determined to do it. Sampson did not have a clue or maybe he did and decided to ignore the prior attacks on his life. Believing he could continually take the anointing on his life for granted by playing with fire and not be burned. We women tend to do that a lot! Sampson was displaying "silly" behavior. He falls for her tears and cunning words. You know the ones we hear from men, "I love you," and "Baby, I would never hurt you." Sampson spills his guts about what makes him strong and finds himself with no eyeballs, no hair, and no strength. Messing around with his ideal woman destroyed him and in the end, he died with her and her Philistine crew. Delilah name means "one who weakened, uprooted or impoverished. She did what her name described!

One day I watched an episode of Cheaters where a woman in her mid fifties called the show to investigate her husband. They followed him for a few weeks and confronted her with the evidence. She explained that she was a Christian and that she took her marriage vows to heart. She said her husband had cheated on her before with women in her church and her co-workers. She was tired of his mess after twenty years and wanted it to stop. The host of the show revealed that her husband and the other woman were at their home. He asked would she like to confront them. She said yes. Upon arriving at their home her husband was standing at the front door, probably looking out for her. She was supposed to be at a church function. She approached him and told him she knew all about his affair. He shrugged her off by asking who these people with her were. She punched him in the face and pushed past him. She walked down the hallway and saw the other woman coming out of their bedroom butt naked! She jumped on the woman and knocked her into the hall closet. By this time, her husband was behind her. She turned on her husband and punched him in his face again. He said that he did not know the woman and that she randomly knocked on their front door requesting to use the bathroom. He told his wife he did not know why this woman was naked. During the update segment, the host revealed that the wife believed her husband. She said she knew when her husband was lying and she believed he was telling the truth. She decided to stay with him. This is a prime example of a "silly" woman. Her husband was caught red handed in her house with another woman who by the way was naked! How much more evidence did she need?

This is how we women waste our lives. This man is not going to change. She figured that if she caught him on tape it would embarrass him enough to make him stop committing adultery. He will not. He showed no remorse and told her she was supposed to be at church anyway. This woman will go through another twenty years of this and in the end blame God for her marriage not working and her husband's detestable behavior.

Here are a few more ways we as women act silly.

- Disobeying God
- Putting a man before our relationship with God
- Putting a man before our children
- Fornicating
- Having a relationship with a married man
- Buying a man
- Shacking up
- Putting all our time and energy in a man God has rejected for our life

Is this you? If it is, do not take offense. God corrects those he loves. He is an active Father. His wish is to guide us using every area of our lives, as a human father would do. God makes you face the truth and challenge you to look within yourself to see if you want to change or not. Many of us have never had a father or father figure in our lives. Therefore, this confrontation about our silliness may be harsh from God at first. Let me explain.

My stepfather never disciplined me my mother did. When I remarried, my husband wanted to take an active role in my children's lives. When he first disciplined them, I did not appreciate it and I would confront him about it in front of the kids. This was wrong and it caused tension between us. He was neither loud nor abusive in his approach. The authority in his voice made me defensive and I was not use to it. I remember one time after my husband disciplined the kids I had to step into the bathroom and close the door. In that moment, I felt like a lioness and I wanted to slap his face with my paw for messing with my cubs. What I felt scared me and I began to pray for help in this area. A few days later while I was out grocery shopping the Lord let me walk up on a man interacting with his children. I heard the same authority in this man's voice when he was speaking to his children. I realized this was normal and that no child likes discipline from its dad. They know with mom they are able to get away with a lot but with dad, it is a whole other story. God showed me the error of my way of thinking and acting on authority. The spirit of offense left and I no longer resented my husband. God made me face my issue with male authority head on and I had a choice to make. Do I ignore what God is showing me about myself or accept what He is saying and receive freedom? I made the choice to be free for all of us. So, receive God's correction and let it bring true deliverance to your life.

> *For the* LORD *disciplines those he loves, and he punishes each one he accepts as his child."*
>
> *As you endure this divine discipline, remember that God is treating you as his own children. Who ever heard of a child who is never disciplined by its father? If God doesn't discipline you as he does all of his children, it means that you are illegitimate and are not really his children at all. Since we respected our earthly fathers who disciplined us, shouldn't we submit even more to the discipline of the Father of our spirits, and live forever?*
>
> *For our earthly fathers disciplined us for a few years, doing the best they knew how. But God's discipline is always good for us, so that we might share in his holiness. Hebrews 12:6-10 NLT*

I had two strikes against me before I got married. One, the man I married was of my own choosing. Two, I was not a born again believer. None of my immediate family members where saved so they had no wise counsel to give me. My oldest sister comment was, "I don't know why he wants to marry you but if he does then go ahead." My mother told him, "If you don't want to be bothered with her then bring her back to her family." What a way to start a marriage! Now I am married and pregnant. My mom was dying, two of my sisters and a brother were on drugs, and my oldest sister was into herself. My mom died four months after I married and the day after her death I found out my husband was cheating on me with a former high school friend of mine. She called me and told me when she found out I was his wife. It felt as if someone had ripped my heart out! My mind said let him go but my heart said I need him. I did not want to be alone since my mom passed away. In addition, he was there for me when I needed help taking care of my mother. How could I leave him when he was the only one there for me? The enemy used this one for a long time to keep me in bondage! My siblings and I were never close due to the large age gap between us. I had no one to turn to and I did not want to be alone nor raise my child without a father. Therefore, I stayed in the marriage.

Now let me tell you it was not easy. Funeral arrangements were set in order, we were trying to get my nephew home from Iraq, everyone was putting in their mouths worth and my aunt was tripping over my mother's insurance money. To top things off my oldest sister decided to schedule the wake and the funeral on my birthday. The devil meant that day and the following birthdays to come as a day of torment for me. Nevertheless, it was the greatest day of my life because I gave my life to Christ! After the funeral, I still had to deal with the affair and it was extremely difficult for me. I was baptized a few days afterward and I felt like I was truly born again! I knew God had done something wonderful in my life because I felt so clean inside and out. Despite how I felt, I did not have the help and support I needed to get through this difficult time in my life. I did not know I could have gone to the pastor or even how to pray for that matter. Therefore, I went on with life the best I knew how.

The cheating continued and I acted a pure fool because of it. I cut and burned up his clothes in the back yard after seeing Waiting to Exhale. I threatened to bust one of his mistresses over the head with a hot pot of coffee after showing up on his job unexpectedly. In my rage of trying to hurt this woman I accidentally slammed his boss between the door and the wall. This woman looked like a deer caught in headlights when she saw me coming toward her. After the dust settled, I found out that she truly did not know that he was a married man. She apologized profusely and informed me that she was a divorcee herself due to her husband's infidelity. She was a born again Christian, a preacher's daughter and would never knowingly do this to another woman. Then she confronted him concerning his lying about not having a wife and made it clear to him that she would never see him again. True to her word, she never saw him again. We would cross paths from time to time and each time she would ask me if I left him yet. The last time I saw her was at the mall. She remarried and had a beautiful baby. She asked me had I finally left him. I gave her the great news that I had divorced him and moved on with my life. She was very happy for me.

I found out he had another mistress and that he was seeing all three of us at the same time. One night I decided I was going to find him. I did not know exactly which apartment door was hers but I was determined to find out. My cousin happened to see me walking this particular night and asked where I was going. I told him and he drove me to the place where I thought it might be around the corner. I knocked on the door assuming it was her apartment and she answered. When she saw me she slammed the door in my face. I figured she ran to go get him. Sure enough he appears at the door asking me what I was doing there. I told him I was tired of his mess and he walked me out of the hallway into the front of the apartment building. He told me to go home and stop causing trouble. I heatedly told him no. He told me to go home again and when he went to shove me, I turned around and stabbed him three times in the chest with a steak knife. By the grace and mercy of God, it did not penetrate. He went to strike me and my cousin jumped out of his car and warned him not to put his hands on me. The foolishness did not end there!

He broke my television one night with a bat after an intense argument. With that same bat, I hit him in the arm on a different night after he came home from his mistress wanting to argue. He could not use that arm for several weeks. It was just a hot mess! I cut my

hair short to spite him. I cried and begged him to
stay and when that did not work, I tried to kill him
again. I wanted to make him suffer for all the pain
and humiliation I felt. One night, I tied a rope
around his neck while he was asleep and wrapped the
ends of the rope around my hands, as you would do when
you turn double Dutch. When he woke up, he saw me
squatting over him looking out of my mind. The more he
gasped for air the tighter I pulled. While choking him
I heard the Lord say, "Theresa, let him go." I told
the Lord, "No." He said it again, "Theresa let him
go." There was something different about His voice
this time and I knew He was not playing with me. I
released the rope from my hands and jumped off the
bed. He never slept in the same bed with me again. He
slept on the floor facing me at all times.

He would spend his check on his mistress and her
children and leave us with barely anything. Before I
knew he was cheating I had sent him to the store to
pick up a few things. I looked at my receipt upon his
return and saw some extra items on there. I asked him
what happened to these items. He said that there was a
woman standing outside the store with four children
who was asking for money. He told her he could buy
food items for her instead and she said okay. He told
me he knew I would not mind his act of kindness toward
this woman and her children. I agreed with him and
prayed for that woman and her children that night
before I went to bed. I later found out this woman was
his mistress. He even went so far as to tell her that
our second child whom I was pregnant with was not his.
Not only was I devastated upon hearing this lie but
humiliated. Most days I did not know if I was going or
coming. I felt as if I was going to lose my mind. At
this point, I was beyond broken. After this, I had
several turning points.

My first turning point came one day while I was
sitting in his mom's backyard. I had stopped talking
to everyone except my daughter who was three years old
at the time. I told God that I was leaving him
pregnant and all. I did not want my daughter growing

up thinking that it was ok for her husband to cheat on her. I did not want her to think that fussing and fighting was normal behavior between a husband and wife. I did not want her to think this is how a woman is to be treated. I did not care what I had to go through at least I would be free of his tail. True to my word, I left him on the date I gave God. It was not over yet; he called and visited us when he made time. He was trying to have his cake and eat it too. He promised he was coming back to us but never did. He always had an excuse and I believed him. It was as if I had become the mistress and she the wife. I felt it was my duty to continue to be a wife to him even though he had moved to a neighboring state with his mistress and her four children. He was still making booty calls and I felt that as his wife he was due that. Recently, I had a conversation with a friend who was going through this same thing. She was angry that she was not able to have sex with her husband. She felt that it was her right. I shared with her a story I heard on the radio a few years back. A woman called in to get advice on what to do about her cheating husband. Two Christian counselors asked her some questions then gave her advice. These three stuck with me. One cut off all sexual relations with her husband since he continues to exhibit reckless behavior in this area. They warned her about the diseases she could contract from him if she continued to sleep with him. Second, they suggested she seek counseling for herself and any children they may have. They also suggested she ask her husband to go to marriage counseling. If he decided not to go, they advised her to continue to go to counseling on her own. Third, marriage is made of two people not three. Until he give up the other woman there is no marriage. I told my friend if the act of sex is all she wanted that is what she would get. He will be thinking about the other woman and she would be thinking about him having sex with the other woman. Afterward, they would rollover with nothing to say to one another. He will put on his clothes and leave. Leaving her unfulfilled and angry about what just took place.

My second turning point came one day while visiting my niece. She knew all about my problems with my husband. She listened to my foolishness for several months until she could take no more. She told me I was a fool to think he was coming back and I was wasting my time waiting on him to change. She told me that he did not care that the kids and I had no place to live or nothing to eat. She made me face the situation as it was. I listened to all she had to say and when she finished I left. When I got into my car, I called myself telling God on her. "How dare she talk to me that way," I told God. I am her aunt and I helped raise her. She has no right to speak to me in that manner! The Lord told me to shut up. He said that everything she said to me was true and I needed to meditate on it. After a while, I calmed down and thought about what they both said. I called her that evening to tell her thank you. That "love" rebuke changed my life. She cared enough to tell me the truth. Did her rebuke hurt my feelings? Yes. Was she correct in her discernment of my situation? Yes. He is still doing the same mess today.

My last turning point came when I got mad with God and did not speak to him for six months. I would feel his presence and I would let him know I knew He was there but I did not want to talk to him. Still he kept on pursuing me. He said he would leave the ninety-nine and go after the one. One day I was heading to the store to buy some diapers and I felt His presence again. This time I gave in to His wooing and started to cry. I apologized for my behavior toward Him. I cried all the way to the store and he ministered to me. I asked the Lord why he allowed my marriage to break up. I reminded him He has the power to keep it together. Lovingly, He said to me, "I can't make him stay with you when he doesn't want to. Would you want to be with someone who is forced to be with you?" I responded with "No." I learned then if God will not force you against your will there is no need for me to push the issue. I moved on and I cannot tell you how glad I am that I did.

Do you see how silly I was acting? My behavior was sinful (acts of violence, unforgiveness, rage, anger). My thoughts were evil (wanting to kill my ex and make his life miserable as he made mine). I was always learning but never wanting to accept the truth (receiving wise counsel to walk away from a bad marriage but never accepting it). I cannot tell you how many times I have heard stories or seen this behavior on TV. It did not get better for those women. They looked foolish! Still this did not stop me from acting or looking the same. If I had obeyed God when He told me to leave him then I would not have had to go through the extra year of torment. All of my foolish behavior did not bring him home, nor did our daughter crying for him to stay; neither did our unborn child make any difference.

If you are acting silly, there is hope! Get a pen and some paper. Take a few minutes to write down any silly behavior(s) you have expressed concerning a man.

I had you to write them down because I want you to see your behavior on paper. They say hindsight is twenty-twenty. For example when I stabbed my ex husband I was full of hurt and anger. I felt stabbing him would bring me satisfaction or at least it would show him how much he hurt me. This sounds crazy but it is real life stuff.

Next, I want you to write down the consequence(s) that resulted or could have resulted from your behavior. For me the result could have been the death of my ex-husband and a prison sentence for me. My children left in the hands of people who may not have loved, treated, or raised them in the manner in which I would have done. His death would not been worth it. Now, write down what you should or could have done in that situation if you were in the right frame of mind.

The Lord taught me not to make life-changing decisions while emotional, stressed, or sleep deprived. You need to step back from the situation until you have calmed down. When you are in a bad situation, you cannot always see clear, because you are in it. It would not be a bad idea to have your pastor or a trusted friend share with you what they see as an outsider looking in. I also want you to see that staying in a toxic relationship is not worth it! Manifesting ungodly behavior from a bad relationship is not worth it either. I hope that seeing this in writing will help you to move on with your life! Please meditate on this!

A year after my last turning point I was feeling discouraged about my marriage failing and I told God about it. A few nights later, I had a dream I was in my ex-husband's and girlfriend house and it was all white and decorated lavishly. I began to complain to God about how I was living compared to how they were living. The house was beautiful. The house had a spiral staircase and he and his mistress came walking down the stairs. I felt small. I sat on a bench against the wall in their foyer and she came and sat beside me. She seemed upset. All of a sudden, the walls appeared dirty and stained then bondage items started coming out of the walls. I woke up and the Lord said to me that things are not always, as they seem. It may look as if he has it all together but he is in terrible bondage.

He heals the brokenhearted and binds up their wounds [curing their pains and their sorrows]. Psalm 147:3 AMP

When the righteous cry for help the Lord hears, and delivers them out of all their distress and troubles. The Lord is close to those who are of a broken heart and saves such as are crushed with sorrow for sin and are humbly and thoroughly penitent. Psalm 34:17-18 AMP

The Lord knoweth how to deliver the godly out of temptations, and to reserve the unjust unto the Day of Judgment to be punished: 2 Peter 2:9 KJV

I want to end on this note. **I do not condone divorce! God hates divorce and so do I**. I never wanted to divorce my first husband. It rips families apart and leaves a gaping hole where only God can repair, if

the cheating spouse is willing. In my case, he was not
willing and I had to move on. Thank God that all
things work together for the good of those who love
Him. Please take the time to pray and fast, seek wise
counsel and attend pre-marital counseling before
saying I do. Most of all obey the voice of God; it
will save you from so much heartache later.

Chapter 2

WHAT ARE YOU LOOKING FOR

It grieves our Father in heaven when His daughters settle in their choice of a mate because of lack of knowledge, loneliness, low self-esteem, or desperation. It also grieves Him when we have an unrealistic idea of what a man should be. We are looking for the perfect man when there is none. Perfect is being without fault or defect. What we should be looking for and wanting is a man after God's own heart.

Samuel was a prophet in the day of King David. God sent him to the house of Jesse to anoint a new king.

When Jesse and his sons arrived, Samuel noticed Jesse's oldest son, Eliab. "He has to be the one the LORD has chosen," Samuel said to himself.
But the LORD told him, "Samuel, don't think Eliab is the one just because he's tall and handsome. He isn't the one I've chosen. People judge others by what they look like, but I judge people by what is in their hearts." CEV 1 Samuel 16:6-7

After seeing Jesse's seven sons Samuel let him know that God had rejected them. Samuel asks if there is another son and Jesse said David.

"Send for him!" Samuel said. "We won't start the ceremony until he gets here."

Jesse sent for David. He was a healthy, good-looking boy with a sparkle in his eyes. As soon as David came, the LORD told Samuel, "He's the one! Get up and pour the olive oil on his head." Samuel poured the oil on David's head while his brothers watched. At that moment, the Spirit of the LORD took control of David and stayed with him from then on. 1 Samuel 16:12-13 CEV

When I was a babe in Christ, there was a man who attended our church service. He was tall, dark and handsome. The pastor asked him to close out the service in prayer. When he got finished praying I was impressed. "That is the type of man I would like for a husband," I said to myself. Instantly, I heard the Lord say, "Do not judge a book by its cover." The tone of God's voice was serious. A few months later, I found out this, man was not only verbally abusive but also physically abusive to his wife. He was a minister in his church, preaching the gospel and a wolf in sheep clothing. He had a nerve to tell her that she was not a real woman because she did not have their children naturally. That had to break her heart! I met his wife and she was beautiful. She had a wonderful spirit. I will never forget that lesson as long as I live.

We must stop making choices out of our flesh (senses and emotions). This is why many of us are in horrible relationships, which is ungodly and sinful in the eyes of God. We need to make choices by the spirit of God. When you make choices out of your spirit, you are inviting the Holy Spirit to help you make the right choice. Remember the Holy Spirit is in you and walks with you. He is a counselor and a guide to those who will listen. God want us to have the best in a husband and the way to get it is through Him.

After the breakup of my first marriage I decided to write a list of qualities, I wanted in a mate. I felt that I must be specific this time around. I did not want to leave any room for error. The top things on my list were, he must be born again, faithful, honest, and he must be kind to my children and me. He must have beautiful teeth and nice feet. In addition, I wanted us to have the same level of sex drive. Of all the things, I listed there were two things that he lacked and I had a hard time dealing with it at first. It was his feet and teeth. All the other qualities I listed he had which were more important. Yet, I was complaining to God about how I would have to look at his feet and teeth for the rest of my life. The Lord impressed upon my heart that his feet and teeth should not be an issue. These things are fixable, but you cannot fix a person's heart or character.

So, where does this idea of a perfect man come from? This idea can come from many places. It could come from the men in your neighborhood or from the men in your family. For some women their idea of a perfect man comes from books. That is where my idea came from. I would read historical romance novels all the time. The men were brave, honest, loyal, warriors, great providers and fabulous in bed. My favorite romance writers at that time were Johanna Lindsey, Amanda Quick, and Julie Garwood. This was during the Fabio craze, when he was the main model for their covers. What I realize now is the men these women wrote about in their books came from their own imaginations.

Get your paper and pen again. Please keep them for the following chapters. Take a few minutes to write down your idea of the perfect man.

For some women it comes from what they see in the media. We take bits and pieces from different men to make up our perfect man in our mind. For example, I would take the masculinity of Sean Connery, the confidence of Denzel Washington and the looks of Morris Chestnut. The body of Terrell Owens, the intellect of Tavis Smiley and the sense of humor of Martin Lawrence with a touch of Ice Cube and that would be the man of my dreams. If you could make your perfect man, who would it be? Write it down.

The Lord revealed to me that when we do this we set ourselves up for heartbreak. When God do send our "Adam" to us, we will reject him because we have this preconceived idea in our mind of a "perfect" man. Alternatively, we might accept "Adam" but compare him to our idea of what a man should be. These ideals will cause frustration in us and hurt in our men. This will lead to failure in our relationship. No one and I mean no one will ever match this standard! Not even those whom I mentioned. Individually, they all have flaws and if you knew their spouses, they would tell you. Besides, we only see the side Hollywood wants us to see about these men. Would you like your potential mate to compare you to his idea of a woman? I do not think so! Especially if his idea of a perfect woman has Halle Berry's looks, Janet Jackson's body, Gabrielle Union's confidence, Condoleezza Rice intellect and Monique's sense of humor. I know I would not!

I had a daughter in the Lord who said she did not like men with a hairy chest. She said if she got married she would make him shave or wax his chest because she did not want to lay her face on his hairy chest at night. I told her she was crazy because no man in his right mind is going to be shaving or waxing his chest every couple of days to accommodate her warped idea of what a man is suppose to be like. She also preferred white men over black men. It was a plus if they were geeks. I asked her what if God sent her a Harvard educated black man, who was a born again Christian with a hairy chest. She looked like she wanted to vomit. I told her she was going to miss out on her blessing with that messed up mindset of hers. Believe me she is not the only woman who thinks like this!

The bible tells us to cast down our "wild" imaginations and every high thing that exalts itself against the knowledge of God. We do not know what is best for us we only think we do. Does this mean we have to throw all of our wishes out the window and settle for less? No! It means we need to be sensible about our expectations in a man. We need a balance in what God wants for us and what we desire.

In the movie, Shrek there is a scene where Shrek went to rescue Fiona from the fierce dragon. He arrived at her bedside, jerked her up, and ran for safety. She was upset. Where was the kiss he was to lay gently on her lips? During the escape, she hollered and screamed about how long she had waited in that old castle for her knight in shining armor to rescue her and this is what she gets. All Shrek was thinking about was getting them both out of the castle. When they made it to safety and he took off his face armor she almost died. He was not what she had been waiting for at all! He was big, green, and ugly! He was an ogre! Fiona was devastated. That is because she had built up in her mind the unrealistic expectation of what her mate should be. We are not perfect, so why should we demand that our future mate be also? In the end, Fiona fell in love with Shrek for who he was. She realized that Shrek might not have been what she would have chosen for herself, yet he was what she needed.

Write out a list of qualities you desire for your "Adam" to have. Take a few days to pray over your list, talk to God about it, and listen to what He has to say. Erase the qualities that God said are superficial and add the ones He brings to your spirit. Keep in mind that God knows all about your "Adam".

Now I want you to write a list of the qualities you posses. Sometimes we think that we have it going on and a man would be crazy not to want to be with us. However, the Father and your "Adam" might not agree. You need to ask the Father what qualities you need to posses to be a good wife, mother, lover and friend. Follow the same instructions as you did for your "Adam" list. Finally, accept that God knows what best for you and trust He will not steer you wr

Lastly, your future husband will not be pe he will have a past. Even you have a past! willing to sit down, hear him out concern' and not be judgmental. If he has moved on and consistently lived a life totally opposite of his past then give him a chance. **This is only if the Holy Spirit leads you. If He tells you to leave this one alone, please do so.** However, do not sit across from this man with your nose up in the air as if you never done anything wrong in your life or never did something that made you feel ashamed.

Chapter 3

ARE YOU READY

Almost all women think that they are ready to move forward in a relationship. In spite of that, after reading this chapter you may think again. If you are married, you are not ready. You are not even qualified! If you are separated from your ex and do not have your certificate of divorce, you are not ready. Some women tend to think separation mean they are divorced. In God's eyes, you are still married and if you get involved or are involved with another man, you are committing adultery.

The Lord led me to call a friend one day to see how she was doing. She told me she had met this man and had gone out on two dates with him. She said that she did not think it would work because he seemed to be detached emotionally. I asked her to explain. She said after dinner on the first date they watched movies while laying on the floor and she laid her head on his shoulder. She said he did not respond to her display of affection. I told her you only had two dates, how did you want him to respond. She went on to say how she likes to laugh and have a good time and she needs someone who is like her. She needs someone who is affectionate and family oriented. I told her that I understood where she was coming from but maybe that is the problem; wanting someone just like herself. She then said that she thought it was strange the way he can stay in the house all day by himself. She found that to be weird. I explained to her that some people like spending time by themselves. It is a problem for you because you are afraid to be alone. It offended her that he thought she asked too many questions. "His observation is true", I told her. She said she does this because she deals with grown folk who act like children on a daily basis. I let her know that this is a real man you are dealing with and he may feel you are being too personal especially only after two dates. In addition, she did not like the authority in his voice when he talks. I told her that she is so use to being the man in a relationship that when she encounters a real man she is put off. He does not need her asking him questions as if she his mother. She laughed at me and told me she should be able to ask him what she likes. I told her I detected the spirit of Jezebel operating in her. In frustration, she told me again that I did not understand. I told her to move on if she felt so strongly about it. Besides, you are not supposed to be dating anyone in the first place. You are still married. She got upset and told me that she felt it was unfair that her husband could be with another woman and she left by herself. She wanted to know where the justice was in that. I let her know because she belongs to God she is held to a higher standard. God wants us to do things decent and in order. It does not matter what someone else does. You can only account for your behavior. Your husband does not have a relationship with God so there is no standard for him. He can live like the devil if he likes.

She was still not satisfied with my answer so I shared with her about the time I was first separated from my ex-husband. His sister and my niece wanted me to stop mopping over him, go out, and meet someone new. After their constant prodding, I went out with them to a club. Every man that asked me to dance I turned down until finally they told me the next man that comes I must dance with him. Sure enough, a very attractive man asked me to dance and I agreed. I felt out of place, not because I could not dance but because my mind was on my broken marriage. It did not help that I was talking to God the whole time in my mind. He brought me back to my table and we talked for a bit. He asked could we exchange numbers. I said sure. He said that he would call me but I hoped he would not. My thought at the time was I am a single woman with two children living with her mother-in-law. I had no job and nothing I could contribute to any relationship. My esteem was beyond low at the time. He called me the next day and wanted to come and see me after work. After making up several excuses at first, I finally agreed. He showed up and he was dressed to kill. I introduced him to my in-laws and my children. We sat and chat for a bit but I felt so uncomfortable. It was not anything he did or said but it was I. I was not emotionally ready to be involved again with another man and I was still married. He called me a few more times but I did not answer or return his calls. It would not have been fair to bring baggage from my marriage into a relationship with him. Besides, I should not have taken advice from people who were not saved, even though they meant well. She said people had been giving her the same advice. I asked her have she ever heard of the song, "Bag Lady" by Erykah Badu. She said yes. I told her she is carrying too much baggage and she needs to let it go.

If you are still longing in your heart after your first love, or the one who got away or the one who broke your heart, you are not ready. If you are dating, a man you know is not right for you, you are not ready. If you have been told that he is not "the one," you are not ready. One day the Lord spoke to me and said, "Why does Nicole keep trying to make me accept someone I have rejected for her." I responded, "What do you mean." He said, "She keeps praying to me about this man being her husband and I told her he is not. She keeps trying to dress him up for me when I have rejected him." God know the heart of man we do not. Man shows us what he want us to see and that is where we make our mistake every time. Unless the spirit of discernment manifests in us and sometimes even after God shows us a person's heart we ignore what He has revealed. We continue to deal with the person rather than move on.

If you are still holding on to love letters, pictures, videos, voice messages, text messages, his clothes, and gifts you are not ready. I was in church one day, and the pastor started talking about someone having love letters in a box on the top right side of their closet. The pastor went on to say if they would get rid of them, God would send whom He had for them. I knew he was talking to me and when I got home, I ripped up every letter in that box and threw it in the dumpster outside. If you hear a song on the radio or listen to a CD that reminds you of him and you get all emotional, you are not ready. If thinking of him makes you reminisce on the love you once had, you are not ready. If you want to be married to appease your flesh, you are not ready. If you are having sex with him, you are definitely not ready.

It is a waste of time to bring another man into your life when you are full of your ex or past relationship(s). You do not have room for him! Go get an empty cup (take the book with you). This cup will represent you. Fill the cup with water. The water represents the man you may have in your life now. Take another cup and fill it with water. This cup represents God and the water represents your "Adam." Try to pour the water from God's cup into your cup. You cannot do it can you? Get rid of the counterfeit "Adam" and make room for the real one! Besides, it is not fair to your "Adam". What if he is ready to be married and he has to hear about how you need to get a divorce and all the other crazy drama that you have not dealt with. He could be with someone who is ready.

If you are still picking or attracting the same type of man, you are not ready. When we have not taken the time to heal from past relationships, we tend to pick the same type of man over again. I have a friend who was married to a short, round, dark skinned man with a big nose. After her divorce, she would show me pictures of her dates. The men in the pictures all looked like her ex-husband except for the differences in height. She swore up and down that these men looked nothing alike but truly, they did. She even asked my husband if this was true and after looking at the pictures, he agreed. Another time we were discussing men in Hollywood whom we found attractive and again she picked men with big noses. Another issue this friend has is that she will only date black men. I told her she needed to be open to whom God would send her. I asked her what if God sent her a white man with a mixture of both her and God's qualities. She said she would pass. I asked her what if this man was her partner in ministry and the will of God for her life. She said she would have to seek God about it. What is there to seek God about? Is she really willing to let some cream in her coffee ruin a chance of true love, happiness and a partner in ministry?

Another friend of mine prefers younger men. We were discussing men and she shared with me her type of man. She was attracted to men like T.I. JaRule, DMX and Juvenile. If you do the research on these types of men and the thug life mentality, you will see that they do not possess the qualities of a real man. When I mentioned different types of men to her like Boris Kodjoe, Lance Gross, Common or Lamman Rucker she turned up her nose. She picks boys expecting them to act like men. On the other hand, she may feel like if she invests in them with her love, time, knowledge and money. They will become the man she wants them to be. When this does not pan out, she is disappointed. I believe in her heart she wants a real man but do not know how to receive one.

Write a list of the men you have dated and/or been married to. Then write down their qualities and the reasons why the relationship failed. As you go over the list, you will see similarities between the men you have dated. I hope that this will cause you to question why you pick/date the same type of man. If you are honest with yourself, you will admit that there is something wrong with your thought process when choosing a man. However, do not fear there is deliverance from this type of mindset and it is through renewing your mind. Renewing your mind comes by changing your thoughts, ideas and what you believe to be right to what God say is right in His word. I challenge you to take the time to search the scriptures on what the Lord says about a godly husband, meditate on it often and hide it in your heart, and then you will be off to a great start because now you are in agreement with the word of God concerning this matter. His looks, the manner in which he is dressed or the fancy car he drives will not easily fool you. The word will constantly remind you that you need more than the superficial!

If you allow God to renew your mind in this area, you will be able to have the marriage you desire.

If you have not gotten over any type of issues concerning your father, you are not ready! During a service, a pastor shared her childhood with us. She said that her father was a man of the streets who abused her mother but did not abuse her. She loved him with all of her heart but things were always a mess at home. When she became an adult, she chose men that reminded her of her father. She married men who were drug abusers and abusive. She made them co-pastors and bishops of her church thinking that if she could clean them up and get them saved, everything would be all right. It did not. She encouraged us not to follow her example.

If you are still dealing with issues of any kind of abuse, lack of trust, abandonment, rejection, rape or molestation you are not ready. If your self-esteem is so low that you have to be reassured constantly that he loves you, you are not ready. Your constant neediness and/or clinginess will make him not want to be around you. If you are bitter, wanting to make all men pay for what one man did to you in the past, you are not ready. If you are jealous, controlling, manipulative, mean-spirited, or just plain evil, you are not ready.

Say you are still dealing with the spirit of rejection. The first time your man tell you he is

going to hang out with his boys you will take that as
him rejecting you. You will start a big argument to
make him feel guilty. He will stay to calm you down
and make you happy but he will feel miserable. How
long do you think this will work? The issue is not
him. It is you! This recently happened to a young
woman I know. My husband wanted to take her boyfriend
to shoot some hoops. I will call this young woman
"Pat." Pat got mad and threw a tantrum. She told him
he did not need to go play basketball. She was cutting
up so bad he decided to stay and play Monopoly with
her. My husband and our kids joined the game. Near the
end of the game, she got very upset because he sold my
husband his properties and she thought he should have
given them to her. She carried on so, he said he
wished he had never played the game. The next day I
spoke to her about her behavior and she admitted that
she did not want him out of her site. I explained to
her how her insecurities could ruin their
relationship. She understood and said she would work
on it.

Ladies, we must take the time to heal. We slap a
band-aid on a gaping wound and hope that it do not
bleed, ooze or smell and keep on going. On the other
hand, some do not touch the wound at all, hoping it
heals by itself. We think to ourselves maybe no one
will notice it. If I pretend, nothing is wrong maybe
they will also.

When I was a teenager, I had an abscess that needed
surgery. I did not want to go to the emergency room. I
was afraid and I did not know what to expect. I had a
party set for that Friday night and all day at school,
my behind was on fire. I had to sit on my side because
I could not sit flat in the chair. I drove my car
while leaning on my hip. You know that had to be
awkward. I was popping Tylenols as if it was going out
of style. It did not help. I ignored the pain and
danced the night away. The following morning I was in
so much pain. My mother cussed me out for acting so
foolishly and then took me to the hospital. I had the
procedure done and went home. I did not know how
painful the healing process would be. I could not walk

for about a week or two. I could only sleep on my sides. I could not bathe the first week or so, just wash up. My mom and my sister had to take turns removing my packing and inserting a fresh one. They had to make sure the wound was clean at all times. It was not an enjoyable experience for me and I know it was not one for them either. I finally healed and all I have to show for it is a scar of what happened in my past.

Maybe your abscess that need surgery is getting a divorce, finally breaking it off with a boyfriend, dealing with rejection, renewing your mind or abuse issues. You need to get that thing lanced and let all that "pus" out of you. Let the Great Physician take out your old packing and put in new packing. You must keep your wound cleaned daily with "spiritual antiseptic," the word of God. Follow the Holy Ghost orders until there is no more pain and only a scar left of what use to be. Then you will be ready to receive whom God has for you.

You might be asking yourself, "How long will the healing process take"? It all depends on how bad your situation is and if you are willing to do whatever the Holy Spirit ask of you and complete it. For example, what if when the pastor spoke that word about the love letters being in the top of someone closet and knowing he was talking about me I did not go home and get rid of them. As long as it took me to get rid of those letters would be however long it would take me to go to that next stage of healing or getting my "Adam."

There are two hindrances in the healing process. The first hindrance is fear. The devil told me many times I would never make it through the separation and divorce. He even told me no man would marry me with two children. It got so bad during the separation that I made up in my mind to kill my daughter, my unborn son and myself. I went to a park to do the deed. While sitting on the riverbank waiting for my daughter to finish her food so I could grab her and jump in the river, an Angel of the Lord came and sat down beside me and said, "You will not kill yourself, or your children." His presence was so overwhelming that I

43

started to weep uncontrollably and he ministered to me until I got myself together. God is a good God! Do not be afraid to push past the pain and go on with your life. Stop worrying about how you are going to make it without him or if you will ever love again. Do not let fear stop you from going forth in your destiny! Trust God to walk you through the healing process.

The second is refusing to listen and obey. If you are a person who is determined to do it your way, it will take longer. Only when you decide your way is not working and do it God's way will you see a change. Obedience is better than sacrifice.

"How long will you simple ones love your simple ways? How long will mockers delight in mockery and fools hate knowledge? If you had responded to my rebuke, I would have poured out my heart to you and made my thoughts known to you.

But since you rejected me when I called and no one gave heed when I stretched out my hand, since you ignored all my advice and would not accept my rebuke, I in turn will laugh at your disaster;

I will mock when calamity overtakes you- when calamity overtakes you like a storm, when disaster sweeps over you like a whirlwind, when distress and trouble overwhelm you.

Then they will call to me but I will not answer; they will look for me but will not find me.

Since they hated knowledge and did not chose to fear the Lord, since they would not accept my advice and spurned my rebuke, they will eat the fruit of their ways and be filled with the fruit of their schemes.

For the waywardness of the simple will kill them, and the complacency of fools will destroy them; but whoever listens to me will live in safety and be at ease, without fear of harm." Proverbs 1:22-33 NIV

Many of us have no clue of what marriage is about. I will admit I had no clue! Some of us have dreamed about marrying since we were little. As for myself, I never dreamed about getting married. Maybe because of what I saw growing up. I had never even heard the word marriage in my home. If I were to give my definition of marriage back then, it would have gone like this. A man who came home five days out of the week; leaving my mom's groceries out in the car along with her money under the driver's seat mat. A mom who would tie my dad up and beat his knees with a serving spoon because the money he left her came up short. I saw no hugs, no kisses, and no normal communication between them. I also had aunts and uncles who were married for over forty years but I never saw any love or tenderness between them. Not even my sibling's marriages stayed together. No wonder my first marriage failed! I was not prepared. I did not know I should fast and pray about such a major decision. I did not know God needed to be the head of a marriage. I did not know anything about love, forgiveness, communication, respect, and honor. If this sounds similar, you are not ready.

Even before you enter elementary school there is pre-school. This prepares children for what school is going to be like before they get there. There are many benefits to pre-school. Children learn some independence from their parents, they learn how to interact and get along with other children. They learn structure in the classroom. They learn their role as a student as well as the teacher's roll in the classroom. They learn to take authority from another adult besides their parents.

God has made this same provision for you! If you ask the Holy Ghost, He will show you what books to read, how to pray and/or pray and fast. He will show you who to seek counsel from and where to go to get what you need. He did it for me and I know He will do it for you!

But the Comforter (Counselor, Helper, Intercessor, Advocate, Strengthener, Standby), the Holy Spirit, Whom the Father will send in My name [in My place, to represent Me and act on My behalf], He will teach you all things. And He will cause you to recall (will remind you of, bring to your remembrance) everything I have told you. John 14:26 AMP

Now does this mean you will know everything about marriage? No. Does this mean your marriage will be perfect? No. Yet, you will be ready for the beginning stages of marriage. The rest you will learn as you live the married life and by allowing the Holy Spirit to teach you as you go along. Let me part with this final story to better illustrate my point of being ready.

I know a young woman whom God had been trying for three years to prepare for marriage. During this preparation time, she refused to listen to wise counsel, read the suggested books, or follow the instructions of the Holy Ghost. She did not want to do the work necessary to receive healing. When a man showed up, she was not ready. She was still dealing with trust issues. This young man was ready to be married and was willing to have her relocate to where he lived. As the relationship progressed, he noticed her issues with trust. After praying about it, the Lord revealed to him that this young woman needed to stay where she was because she was not ready. She admitted that the counseling she received went in one ear and out the other. Now she is scrambling to do the work that she should have done three years earlier. The story does not end here.

I came back in contact with a Prophetess whom I had not spoken to for a year. She inquired about this young woman's well-being and wanted to know if she was dating someone. I told her the young woman was well and that she had a boyfriend. She said she saw trouble all around this young woman but did not go into details to protect her privacy due to us praying in a group. The next day she called me and shared in depth, what the Lord had showed her. In the vision, she saw this young woman boyfriend drive her to a wooded area and drop her off. The young woman was six months pregnant and surrounded by snakes. The woods were all dark and slimy and there was little light in sight. She tried to jump over the snakes but could not due to the pregnancy. The Prophetess suggested that this young woman come out of that relationship and stop shacking up with him. If she chooses to stay with him, she will go through a very rough time but God will deliver her in the end. The seriousness of this word brought confirmation to the trouble I was feeling in my spirit concerning this young woman. On several occasions, I warned her of the uneasiness I was feeling concerning their relationship, due to both of their behavior.

I called this young woman and told her what the Prophetess said. She seemed alarmed and concerned but she could not believe that this man would leave her in that type of situation. While listening to her concerns God gave me a word to give to her. He told me to tell her that she is out of His timing. He went on to explain that when He told her to prepare herself for that time she did not do so and when the man came she was not ready. God went on to explain that the time she spent with him and his mother at his house for a few months was the time they were to be married and for them to become as one. Now she was in another time and things have changed for them both in the realm of the spirit and in the natural. She was upset after hearing this and kept trying to understand why all of a sudden God would change His mind. God had me to remind her again as He had a few times before that she cannot get over, around or under Him, nor can she out think Him. She then went to blame my husband saying that he was the one that told her this man was her husband. I knew that was not true because my husband always kept a level head when it came to their relationship. He even asked her how she knew this young man was her husband and she said, "God told her so while she was in prayer." He politely responded with, "How is it you can hear clearly from God concerning this man being your husband but you are always confused about hearing from God on other matters in your life?" She could give him no reply.

Recently my daughter told me that while on her Facebook page she saw a post of this young woman receiving congratulations on her baby. It did not say whether she had the baby or whether she was still pregnant but I thought about that word God spoke a few months ago. The Lord reminded me about another situation where a woman was warned not to sleep with a certain man in her life because the man would sleep with her then leave her. She thought to herself that this person giving her this word had it wrong. This man in her life loved her and asked for her hand in marriage on several occasions over the years. He even asked for her hand in marriage recently and she was thinking about marrying him. Nevertheless, she heeded the warning from the Lord and did not marry him. After a very short time, this man passed away unexpectedly. She called me with the news and expressed how hurt she was and how messed up she would have been if she would have disobeyed God and married him. She went on to explain how she thought God was talking about him leaving her for another woman, but God was talking about him leaving her by death. As I pondered this in my heart and thought about the young woman's situation, it came to my spirit that this young man does not have to abandon her in the natural in order to abandon her emotionally and mentally. There are many marriages where couples live together married in name only. They sleep in separate bedrooms, sexually, mentally and emotionally detached from one another while parenting any children they may have. The O'Jays song says it best, "Your body's here with me but your mind is on the other side of town." We need to stop being wise in our own eyes and just obey God.

Let me end this story with what God just dropped in my spirit concerning His timing. Say for instance, you and a few friends planned to take a cruise in the summer. You buy your ticket in advance and the date and time is set. All you have to do is prepare yourself within the allotted time to get ready to go. If that means getting a passport, buying new clothes, paying a visit to the doctor or whatever else you need to do in order to be ready for that day. Now on the day you are set to sail, you miss the ship because you took your sweet old time getting ready at home. Now you are standing on the dock watching the ship sail away in the distance. You are mad with your friends for leaving you, the captain because he set sail without you and anyone else you can be mad at all because **you were late**. After you have calmed down you decide that you are going to plan another cruise. You even choose to sail on the same ship hoping you will have the same experience you missed. However, it will be different. Your friends will not be there and there will be a completely new set of people aboard the ship. The weather will be different which will affect the waves of the sea. Your cabin number will not be the same and that probably goes for the crew as well. I will go so far as to say the food will taste different. Even you will be different because a lot can happen to a person within a couple of months. Now do you understand why it is important to move in God's time? This young woman can stay with this man and even marry him (which she did). She can do everything in her power to make it work but the relationship will never be what (or sail) as God originally intended. God did not change His mind; she just missed the timing of God.

Write down examples you have seen of a loving marriage. Then search the bible to find out what God has said about love, marriage, and sex. Write down the scriptures He give you and meditate on them often. If your examples of a loving marriage do not line up with the word of God then, you do not want to imitate them. You want to model you marriage after the word of God.

Write down the things you know you need God to work on emotionally, spiritually and physically in your life before you say, "I do." After doing so take the time to pray over them, obey God's instructions and believe Him to deliver you and bring healing in your life.

Father in the name of Jesus, I come before your throne of grace humbly as I know how. You know the heart is wicked and utterly defiled who should know it but you. I ask you on this day to show me any relationships I have been in that where unclean and not pleasing to you. I ask that you cleanse, purge and deliver me from the effects of past relationships and wipe away the residue. Father, I ask that you sever and break every

unhealthy soul-tie because of those relationships. I
stand in faith and count it done in your son Jesus
name, Amen.

Chapter 4

STOP IGNORING THE WARNING SIGNS

Often I hear after a woman breaks up with a man, "I didn't know he was like that" or "He didn't act that way before we were married." I have found this to be untrue. We see the warning signs but blatantly ignore them. We think our love, beauty, and sex can change a man and it cannot. If a man is beating you before the marriage, it will continue afterward. If he is a drug abuser, he will be one after the marriage. If he cheated on you while dating and you put up with it, he will do it throughout the marriage. No amount of love, sex, or begging will cause this man to change; only the saving power of Jesus Christ can bring about change. I am not talking about your relationship with Christ but he has to have his own personal relationship with the Lord. If he does not then change will never take place until he does! You will pay a price going through with this man and is it a price you are willing to pay? Take the story of Leah in the bible.

Now Laban had two daughters. The older daughter was named Leah, and the younger one was Rachel. There was no sparkle in Leah's eyes, but Rachel had a beautiful figure and a lovely face. Since Jacob was in love with

Rachel, he told her father, "I'll work for you for seven years if you'll give me Rachel, your younger daughter, as my wife." Genesis 29:16-18 NLT

So Laban invited everyone in the neighborhood and prepared a wedding feast. But that night, when it was dark, Laban took Leah to Jacob, and he slept with her. (Laban had given Leah a servant, Zilpah, to be her maid.)

But when Jacob woke up in the morning—it was Leah! "What have you done to me?" Jacob raged at Laban. "I worked seven years for Rachel! Why have you tricked me?"

"It's not our custom here to marry off a younger daughter ahead of the firstborn," Laban replied. "But wait until the bridal week is over, then we'll give you Rachel, too—provided you promise to work another seven years for me."

So Jacob agreed to work seven more years. A week after Jacob had married Leah, Laban gave him Rachel, too. (Laban gave Rachel a servant, Bilhah, to be her maid.) So Jacob slept with Rachel, too, and he loved her much more than Leah. He then stayed and worked for Laban the additional seven years. Genesis 29:22-30 NLT

Laban married Leah off to a man that did not love her nor was he remotely attracted to her. Despite the rejection from Jacob and the fact she had no choice about leaving; she tried her best to make the marriage work. God saw that Leah was unloved so he caused her to conceive. She had her first son, named Reuben, and said, *"The LORD has noticed my misery, and now my husband will love me."* She had a second son named Simeon and said, *"The LORD heard that I was unloved and has given me another son."* She had another son named Levi and said, *"Surely this time my husband will feel affection for me, since I have given him three sons!"* Then there was Judah and she said, *"Now I will praise the LORD!"* Leah concluded after having several babies with Jacob it was not going to happen. He did not even feel any affection toward her. Now that is sad! He loved Rachel and no amount of male heirs she had changed it. You have the choice to move on.

During the end of my first marriage, I made up my mind to leave my husband. He was cheating on me and I had enough. I remember sitting in my mother-in-law's backyard and I told God I was leaving him. I gave God a date and I told him I did not care what I had to go through long as I was away from him. True to my word, I left. He was shocked when he came home and saw only the bedrails left. It did not end there. I allowed him to play mind games with our daughter and me over another year. This was after God had warned me to move on. He promised to come home and each time it never happened. When he did visit, he wanted to have sex with me. I was pregnant with our second child and I thought it would be wrong to deny him since I was still married to him. After sleeping with him, I would always feel dirty as if I was the other woman. I did not enjoy this feeling and I stopped sleeping with him. When I would ask him for help financially, he would always tell me he did not have any money. God in his goodness spoke to my heart and said, "Do not call or ask him for anything else, I will provide." True to his word, God did and I never had to call him for nothing! God is good! Sisters, God will take care of you when your husband rejects you!

For your Maker is your Husband-the Lord of host is His name-and the Holy One of Israel is your Redeemer, the God of the whole earth He is called.

For the Lord has called you like a woman forsaken, grieved in spirit, and heart sore-even a wife [wooed and won] in youth, when she is [later] refused and scorned, says your God. Isaiah 54: 5-6 AMP

A Pastor friend of mine involved herself with a man (a pastor also) who was married even though he had been separated for three years. While they were dating, he started the divorce proceedings. During this time, she called my husband for counseling with him on the line. After praying for them my husband felt he was not ready to be married again. He felt that this man still loved his first wife and he needed some time to heal and maybe some counseling would help. Several other pastors and prophets told her he was not the one as well. They married anyway and it

got ugly fast. One day his ex-wife showed up
unannounced at their home, words were exchanged
between them and my friend punched his ex-wife in her
mouth. After the fight her husband took the side of
the ex-wife and told my friend he did not love her and
he thought it best she leave. My friend refused to go.
She continued to plan the wedding reception and the
honeymoon trip as if nothing happened. She also found
letters from the former wife asking him to stop
cheating on her. She wanted him to clean up and stop
being a pack rat. She went through this for nineteen
years. Even after reading this, my friend still blamed
his ex-wife for the state of this man. She was going
through the same stuff he did with his first wife.
Yet, she refused to hear or see the truth.

About a month later, another fight occurred when she
found out he was still paying his ex-wife's car note
and insurance. She confronted him on it and he refused
to discuss it. In frustration, she pushed him a few
times and on a last push, he charged her and choked
her. She got him off her when she reached for a knife.
He called the police and again he told her he did not
love her and wanted her to leave. Again, she refused!
I asked her to leave but she would not listen. She
said because she was his wife she had a right to stay.
She was not leaving until he paid her to leave. She
blamed God for bringing them together and she could
not understand why God would send him to her. In
anger, she said a prison ministry would be fine with
her. Sister's, no man is worth a prison ministry!

After the above incident, she was coming out of the
grocery store and while walking to her car a man
called her name. She looked to see who it was and it
was a man she knew from ministry. He had come into
town to preach a revival and told her he had been
looking for her for about three years. Everyone he
asked said he or she did not know where she was. Right
there on the spot he asked her to marry him and sadly,
she had to tell him she was married. After this
encounter, she had to go home to the husband who was
taking her through hell. Several years earlier God had
me to tell this pastor that her husband was not from

this area. Sure enough, he was not. The last time I
spoke to her, she asked me to call her back later in
the evening to pray for her and some other women who
were going through in their marriage. I told her I
would and forgot about it until the next day. Every
time I went to call her after that, I could not. The
Lord did not give me anything in my spirit to pray.
After about two weeks, the Lord spoke to my heart
about her situation. He told me the reason why I could
not call her back to pray. She wanted me to come in
agreement with her to pray against her husband's will.
This man has made it clear that he has made a mistake
and do not want to stay married. To pray in agreement
with her would have me operating in the spirit of
witchcraft. God did not want me to have no part in
that. Moreover, I did not know any of those other
women or their situation. Why do we think we can save
the day and change a man's lifestyle? She knew when
she started dating him that he was a packrat. She saw
how he lived when she visited his house. We foolishly
make this same mistake over and over again.

Another Pastor friend of mine married an unbeliever.
She felt because they did not have sex before they
were married God would honor it. This man was violent
and abusive toward her. She kept trying to convince my
husband and me that he was a man of God because he did
praise and worship with her. She then tells me that he
told her when he does praise and worship with her it
feels as if someone is beating him upside his head.
How can this be? Can a man who she claimed is saved
abuse her without having any remorse? If the Holy
Ghost lived in him, he would listen to what God has to
say and stop abusing her. He would go to counseling
and do whatever it takes to change his behavior. You
will see the change and not just hear he is trying to
change. In addition, it would not feel like someone is
beating him upside the head during praise and worship
if they both served the same God.

He would show her movies about Christians being
defeated by witchcraft workers and that made her fear
him even the more along with the beatings she took
from him. He would take her along with him when he

went to go cop drugs. She would refuse to go with him if he went to buy drugs near her church. She did not want to take the chance of being seen by other members. As she revealed these things to us, she insisted that he was a man of God. When we told her there was no way he could be a man of God she rebuked us. She said that we were in no position to say who is saved and who is not saved. We reminded her that the word of God says, "You shall know them by the fruit that they bear." She refused to listen to a word we had to say. She defended him and his actions at every hand. Hearing and seeing this broke my heart! I tossed and turned many nights because of it. She could no longer pray as she used to. I no longer heard her speak the word of God as before. She was smoking cigarettes now and her anointed singing voice was no longer intact. The most devastating thing that I heard from her was that she was beginning to believe you could live anyway you wanted to and still go to . heaven. This was because she truly believed in her heart that her husband was a man of God and she never saw God correct or rebuke him concerning his behavior toward her.

Before she married him, she received a prophetic word from her spiritual mother in the Lord. She gave her the description of the man, that he would beat her and her son would end up killing him. Another pastor asked her to wait until he sought God about it. She told me she gave the man of God seven days to pray and when he did not call her back within that timeframe, she married this man anyway. Things happened just as the first pastor said it would. Her son went to kill this man on at least two occasions. The Holy Spirit stepped in and stopped him from ruining his life.

I remember seeing Kirk Franklin on a Christian program talking about his former porn addiction. He said when he became serious about his deliverance and making it right with his wife, he set up his own counseling sessions. He did not request that she go with him to counseling because she did not do anything wrong. The mess that they went through was his fault and he took full responsibility for it. He took measures to make sure he was held accountable. Their marriage stayed together because he proved to his wife and God that he wanted it to work. Along with his wife prayers, the prayers of others and his commitment to the marriage, God worked it out for them and I praise God for that!

When women stay in abusive relationship's it means they do not value themselves. When a person feels they have value they will not allow anyone to abuse or mistreat them. You must love yourself enough to move on!

A friend of mine confided in me she was leaving her husband. She said she never should have married him. The Lord recently told her she was connected to the wrong wire. She asked the Lord to explain. He told her when you build a house you have electrical wiring installed to make sure all appliances work in your home. If you put two wires together that do not belong it can cause a short or even a fire. If you put two wires together that belong there will be none of that. Your wires have shorted out that is why the marriage is not working. Your wires never belonged together. Five months after that revelation she found out he was cheating on her. She called me to pray and fast with her as the Lord led me. I prayed for her but I was waiting on the Holy Ghost to pray through me about this situation. About two weeks later after waking up from a nap the Lord gave me this word for her. He told me to tell her the reason why she does not have the things she desires is because of the people around her. If she would let the people go around her that would free up her money and she would be able to have the house, car, or any other thing she desires. After telling her this, she told me every time she and her husband went somewhere he had to bring someone else with them. Someone was always living with them and she was tired of that. The Lord told me to tell her to stop being afraid to be and live alone. God would be with her. She said she did not want to disappoint God. I told her God is trying to do a new thing in her life and she needs to allow Him to do it. He also told me to tell her not to buy her husband another thing. She started laughing and told me that when they received their income taxes back it all went to him and she bought nothing for herself.

She called me back a few weeks later very distraught threatening to burn down his mother and mistress houses. She was very upset because she had been deceived. The money she would give him to help feed him and his mother he gave to his mistress and her children. She also found out his mistress was the neighborhood prostitute. Now she has to worry and wait for test results to make sure she is disease free. The icing on the cake is that his mistress is pregnant. She confessed that she did not believe what I told her God said. She said it did not line up with the word of God and that God would not tell you to stop helping your husband. I told her I understood but God knew what he was doing all the time.

Why do we blame God in one way or another for the mess we made ourselves? God is not to blame. We disobeyed His word and the warnings He sent. We must take responsibility for your own actions, repent, make it right with God, and come out of sin.

Let no man say when he is tempted, I am tempted from God; for God is incapable of being tempted by [what is] evil and He Himself tempts no one. But every person is tempted when he is drawn away, enticed and baited by his own evil desire (lust, passions). Then the evil desire, when it has conceived, gives birth to sin, and sin, when it is fully matured, brings forth death. James 1:13-15

God is a forgiving God, turn to Him, and let Him restore you!

All whom My Father gives (entrusts) to Me will come to Me.; and the one who comes to Me I will most certainly not cast out [I will never, no never, reject one of them who comes to Me] John 6:37 AMP

Chapter 5

I AM AFRAID TO LIVE ALONE

In Genesis 1 and 2 God created Adam and placed him in the Garden of Eden with instructions for his life. Adam's life had a purpose; to have dominion (supreme authority) over all God created. Yet, God saw that Adam was alone and decided to make a helpmate for him. In the meantime, God had another purpose for Adam. As God formed living creatures out of the ground, he brought them before Adam and he named them. This had to take a longtime with the variety of animals we have here on earth. After this, God blessed Adam with his wife.

Adam was alone but he was not lonely. He had a relationship with God and he was so full of purpose that he did not even know he needed a wife. The Lord explained to me the reason women are afraid to be or live alone is because they have no purpose. The definition of *purpose is an object or* result aimed at *or* achieved. Purpose causes you to get up in the morning with expectancy so you can look forward to your day. When you do not have a purpose, you look to things and people to fulfill you. Moreover, women think having a man will fulfill them. So, without a purpose they spend all of their time either looking for a man or holding on to a sorry excuse for one. Either way there is no fulfillment. Yet, they choose to live in fornication with a man than live alone and find out what God's purpose is for their lives.

Living alone helps you to learn more about yourself. When the Lord blessed me with my place, I admit I was scared. I had lived with my family till I was twenty-one then with my first husband. After we divorced, I lived with his mom and sister for a while. Therefore, here I am at twenty-eight with two children living alone. For a couple of months I stayed mostly in the bedroom then I began to venture out to the rest of the apartment. I learned to enjoy it. I was able to cook and experiment with new recipes. I decorated my apartment the way I liked. I played my music as loud and long as I wanted. I raised my children the way I wanted without people's interference. I did not have to worry about coming home to find my food eaten or my money stolen. I had a bathroom that I did not have to clean before my kids and I used it. I prayed as much as I needed to and read my bible anytime I felt like it. I did not have a trifling man living with us telling us what to do.

Most of all God used this time of living alone to reveal more of my purpose to me and to get me ready for my future. During this time, the Lord unveiled my writing gifts. You can use this time in your life to go back to school, learn how to cook, start the business that you always dreamed of, learn a new language, take an art class or take a well- needed trip. My prayers of intercession increased as well as the gift of prophecy. You can spend more time with God in prayer. You can study and read the word of God without interference. He prepared me for my husband. He taught me how to be a wife and a mother. He never abused me or mistreated me. He corrected me when I needed it. He encouraged me and believed in me. He was and is my example of a husband. There was so much peace in my home and I enjoyed it. God kept me and he will do it for you if you allow Him too. Sure, I got lonely at times but God was there. He also surrounded me with older women in the Lord to love on me and guide me in the right direction. Yes, I talked to men in general and I wanted male companionship but I was determined to live holy before God. I tried hard not to put myself in positions that would cause me to sin against God. Most of all I prayed earnestly for God to keep me all the time and He did.

Please hear me! God know you desire a mate but He does not want just anybody for your husband! While writing this I asked God why he took a rib from Adam to make Eve and not a part of his heart. He told me to look up rib in the dictionary. When I looked it up, I did not find anything that caught my attention. He said, "Look up bone." I did and still nothing. "What's inside the bone," he asked. I said, "Marrow." He said look it up. I did and the first definition said "a soft vascular tissue that fills the cavities of most bones." The second definition said, "Heart; core." When I looked in my son's encyclopedia, it said inside the marrow is where blood and cells are formed. Cells are the foundational units of life. My son's encyclopedia defined blood as a river of life flowing through your body. One definition of core was defined as a central or most important part. God took the most important part of Adam and placed it in Eve. That is why after Adam woke up he said:

This is now bone of my bones, and flesh of my flesh: she shall be called Woman, because she was taken out of Man. Therefore shall a man leave his father and his mother, and shall cleave unto his wife: and they shall be one flesh. And they were both naked, the man and his wife, and were not ashamed. Genesis 2:23-25

You best to believe Eve had no problem with that! She knew she came from Adam. This is why relationships fail because men are not with their "Eve" and women are not with their "Adam"!

Stop wasting your talents, gifts, and time. Get rid of that man living or coming back and forth in your home! You do not have to be afraid to live alone. God will keep you and protect you. He will provide for your needs. He will package your emotions and sexual urges in a heart shaped box and lay them on his altar.

When that heart shaped box starts to move or jump Jesus will begin to pray and make intercession for you. Lies told to you all of your life will be exposed. He will change the way you see yourself. He will change your mind-set and you will see life through the eyes of Jesus. When it is time, he will do for you as he did for Adam.

Michelle McKinney Hammond had a job singing commercial jingles. Yet, her job was not her purpose. Her purpose came forth out of being single and she obeyed God to write about it. She was so busy fulfilling her purpose that she was not concerned about not being married. That does not mean she does not want to be but she chooses to wait on the Lord. Check her books out. She has a wealth of wisdom and information for the single woman. Jesus knows what it is like to be alone and be lonely. He understands your fear of living alone. I know what it feels like to want a man to validate you. The spirit of rejection and abandonment causes us to be needy and even desperate for love. The blood of Jesus has given us power against these spirits. The spirit of fear has kept us in bondage for long enough. Our Father has delivered us out of the kingdom of darkness and transferred us into the kingdom of light.

Father I come to you in Jesus name confessing that I am afraid to be and live alone. I admit that I have sought fulfillment in men and other things. You said in your word that you are a jealous God and that I should have no other gods before you. I confess that I have put my wants and needs before you and I repent of my sins of idolatry, selfishness, lust, fear, and fornication, in Jesus name. Give me the strength and boldness to clean house and to tell whom I must that it is over and I must be about my Father's business. Lord, reveal your purpose for my life that I may fulfill it. In Jesus name, I pray Amen!

Chapter 6

SEX

Don't you know that your bodies are part of the body of Christ? Is it right for me to join part of the body of Christ to a prostitute? No, it isn't! Don't you know that a man who does that becomes part of her body? The Scriptures say, "The two of them will be like one person." But anyone who is joined to the Lord is one in spirit with him.

Don't be immoral in matters of sex. That is a sin against your own body in a way that no other sin is. You surely know that your body is a temple where the Holy Spirit lives. The Spirit is in you and is a gift from God. You are no longer your own. God paid a great price for you. So use your body to honor God. 1 Corinthians 6:15-20 CEV

Sex is a wonderful gift from God. It is unique and beautiful. God designed sex for a man and a woman in holy matrimony. I have tasted sex outside of marriage and always felt empty and unclean after doing so. The physical act never failed to please me yet, I desired more and I did not know what the more was. Even after I married my first husband, I felt the same way. Now I realize it was because the men I had slept with was not who God had planned for me. It was only after I married my second husband I did not feel empty or unclean. It was great! While being intimate with my husband on one occasion I heard the Lord say, "I am pleased with your intimacy." That blew my mind! I was happy that my Father was pleased with us.

Drink water from your own well—share your love only with your wife.
Why spill the water of your springs in the streets, having sex with just anyone? You should reserve it for yourselves. Never share it with strangers.

Let your wife be a fountain of blessing for you. Rejoice in the wife of your youth. She is a loving deer, a graceful doe. Let her breasts satisfy you always.
May you always be captivated by her love. Why be captivated, my son, by an immoral woman, or fondle the breasts of a promiscuous woman?

For the LORD sees clearly what a man does, examining every path he takes.
An evil man is held captive by his own sins; they are ropes that catch and hold him. He will die for lack of self-control; he will be lost because of his great foolishness. Proverbs 15:15-23 NLT

You can get several things from the physical side of sex: a good feeling, a bad feeling, a baby, STD's and even death. Yet, no one ever talks about the spiritual and emotional side of sex. Did you know that when you sleep with a man who is not your husband you become one not only in body with him, but in spirit also? Did you know that unclean spirits from that encounter could attach themselves to you? I did not know this either until God revealed it to me. During my separation from my ex husband I was still sleeping with him thinking it was my duty as his wife. I began to have these feelings as if I wanted to strip for him. This was not something that I thought I would do to spice up our marriage. This was different. I had never had these feelings before. I went with those feelings and decided to go spend the little money I had to buy a sexy outfit for him. I went to the dollar general and found this tie-dyed shirt and I brought a pair of bikini underwear to match one of the colors in the shirt. You may be asking yourself what in the world could I have found in the dollar general that would be remotely sexy. Nothing at all, but I was desperate! I would have made anything work to keep my marriage together. I can laugh about it now but back then, it was not funny! He came over and I did my thing for him. He treated me as the stripper I was acting. He took care of his business and went back to his mistress. I was ashamed and felt like I was the mistress and not the wife. I never slept with him again after that. God explained to me that what I was feeling was not me. What had attached to me was the spirit of one of his mistress's. He opened a door that left me open to spiritual attacks. If this could happen to me while married, imagine what happens to the fornicator.

When you fornicate, you come into an unholy covenant with the man or men you slept with and with Satan. You become one in flesh and in spirit, and then a soul-tie takes place. This then gives Satan the legal right to rule over you in the realm of the spirit. This in turn will manifest in the physical realm. Satan is now ruling you undercover and you do not even realize it. This is how women who have never done drugs nor had any desire to do so, all of a sudden start doing drugs. Your soul is now tied to that drug spirit operating in him. Maybe your man's addiction is to alcohol or he could be dabbling in something else. Whatever it is, the same principle applies. This is why when you decide to leave him it is difficult. A chain in the spirit realm is tied to you and every time you try to walk away, you are yanked back. Do you really think Satan is going to let you go that easy? Let us look at this in the natural. Have you ever seen a dog tied to a tree? The owner only gives the dog enough leeway in the chain to feel like he has some freedom but he really do not. The chain hinders the dog from escaping. This is what is happening to you in the realm of the spirit. The only one who has the power to set you free is Jesus Christ! You must confess your sins, renounce the sexual covenant you entered into with this man and Satan, repent and turn from your wicked way! Ask God to destroy the soul-tie and break the chain that binds you to him.

My deliverance came one night at a Friday night service. My Pastor had a video for us to watch called "No More Sheets." We watched the video and it confirmed what God had told me. Before the video was over I received the infilling of the Holy Ghost with the evidence of speaking in tongues. God cleaned me up supernaturally! I felt empowered to live sexually pure before God. It was a powerful night in the Lord! We did not leave until 5:00am in the morning. God will do the same thing for you if you ask Him!

I read this story about a young woman who friend invited her to a club. Upon arriving at the club this friend introduced her to a man she knew. After the club closed, she took this man back to her place and slept with him. A few days later strange things started happening in her apartment. Objects began to move on their own. Daily she was attacked by something she could not see. After a few months of this, she could take no more. She went to see a pastor to try to get help. Each time she went, she could not seem to tell him what happened to her. He earnestly prayed for her deliverance and on the breakthrough visit, the Lord revealed to him what went down. The pastor told her the man she slept with was a warlock. By sleeping with this man, she opened herself up to demonic attack. She confessed her sin, repented and God restored her. If God allowed us to see what takes place in the realm of the spirit when we have sex outside of marriage, we would not be so quick to do so. To see a glimpse of how those demons look and what they do when they enter our bodies would scare us straight. Sex is more than a physical connection!

If the above story seems unreal then think again! A friend of my daughter called her from college asking for prayer. She said a spirit was attacking her in her dorm room. We prayed for her and asked God to keep her safe until she could get home. When she came home the following weekend, she came over our house and shared

with me her story. She told me that all of a sudden
things started moving by themselves in her room. She
said something kept touching her and making noises.
She had not slept in about a week due to what was
going on so she was a wreck emotionally. I asked her
have she been praying and reading the word. She said
yes but that it did not work. She said she slept with
the bible under her head also but the spirit just
keeps on attacking her. The only time it leaves is
when she calls her grandmother on the phone to ask her
to pray. She holds the phone in the air while her
grandmother prays. "When did this activity start?" I
asked her. She said it did not start until after she
went out on a date with this young man. He pursued her
for a while and each time she turned down his
advances. He eventually won her over and she agreed to
go out with him. She said before she got in the car
with him the Holy Spirit told her not to go with him
but she went anyway. "Did you sleep with him?" I
asked. She told me no. I asked her have she dabbled in
the occult recently. She replied again with, "No." I
explained to her the ways in which this type of
activity comes about and she came clean and said she
did sleep with him. She confessed her sin and asked
God to forgive her. We prayed a while longer and after
prayer, she felt better but she was still afraid to go
back to her dorm room. With her permission, we shared
this with her grandmother because she needed someone
to keep her in prayer and hold her accountable. They
both agreed to tell her mother what was going on and
they went the following weekend to pray in the dorm.
She was able to complete her last semester of school
in peace. When you belong to God, you cannot live any
kind of way. We think we can straddle the fence and
not fall off or play with fire and not get burned!
This is just not the case.

We have to stop ignoring God's warnings whether it
is through dreams, by His spirit, from His servants,
or by His word! When I was a sinner, I can remember
when an alarm went off in my spirit not to sleep with
this particular man. I went camping with a girlfriend
of mine. Her boyfriend invited me so that I could keep

his friend company. That night the four of us slept in the same tent. This dude starting rubbing on me and I felt like God was telling me not to sleep with him. I went into the fetal position hoping he would stop touching me. When he did not I tightened my position until eventually he stopped. God allowed me to experience this type of alarm two other times. To this day, I still do not know why! I am not saying God gave me permission to sleep with the other men I slept with in my life. It just shows how powerful God's love, grace and mercy is toward the sinner man. I am glad that I took heed to the Lord's warning even as a sinner! God will not always explain the reason for His warnings. We should just take heed and obey. Should not we as his children be more sensitive to His spirit since we belong to Him?

Sleeping with the wrong man and not being emotionally ready to have sex can lead to disaster. I had a friend when I was a teenager who shared her first sexual experience with me. She said it was a horrible. He was rough and it was very uncomfortable for her. Her window faced the basketball court and the young men playing basketball could hear her crying out in pain. She was ashamed and humiliated. After that experience, she could not bear the thought of having sex again. This type of traumatic experience could affect her for the rest of her life. That young boy cared only about getting in and out and moving on to his next conquest. This is not what God intended for sex between a man and women to be like.

I had a friend who was in an abusive marriage and one day the Lord told me to call her and let her know that if her husband hit her again he would drop dead at her feet. That night he came home in a rage and when he went to hit her, she told him, "If you hit me this will be the last time you hit me again." He calmed down and walked away. Instantly the word of the Lord manifested and she walked with no fear concerning him from that day. One day she called me and asked me to go with her to a club. I told her no. After hanging up I heard the Lord say, "Go with her." I told the Lord, "no." I did not want to go and besides the club was not a place for a Christian woman. He impressed upon my heart that I really needed to go. I called her back and told her to come and get me. Instead of going straight to the nightclub, we ended up in my old neighborhood. She wanted to pick up this man to go with us. I told her this was not the plan and I wanted to leave. She asked could we wait for a few minutes. While waiting I was praying that this dude would not show up. We waited for about fifteen minutes then I told her we were leaving. We went to the club and she danced the whole night while I sat at the table and watched.

The next day I invited her and her children to go to church in the evening to hear my pastor preach. I called my pastor to tell her what happened the night before and she told me the Lord did not tell me to do such a thing. She said I went to the nightclub because I wanted to go. Her words hurt but I knew the Lord impressed upon my heart to go. We went to church that evening and after the service, I went to my car with my sister. My pastor said she would take my friend and her children home. She was still upset with me. While sitting in my car the presence of the Lord came upon me and my sister and I began to worship God. The Lord confirmed He sent me to go with her. He revealed that the man we were waiting on had HIV and if I had not gone, she would have slept with him, contracted the disease, and died. My sister said I needed to go tell her. I got out of my car and went over to my pastor's car to tell her. She began to weep and received the word of the Lord.

At the time, I did not know that the worst was yet to come. One day she called and told me what she was doing and I was shocked. She met men on the internet and would meet them at hotels. It was not just one man; she was meeting several men at one time and having sex with them. She said she just could not stop. She said she tried but it was as if something was pulling her to do it. She said she thought about sex all the time. The spirits of lust and perversion was driving her to sin against her own flesh. I told her if something would have happened to her, we would have been devastated. We would have been wondering how she ended up in a hotel room or in the woods dead. We prayed a pray of repentance together and believed God for her restoration. After I got off the phone I asked the Lord how did this happen. The Lord revealed to me that on the day he released her from fear, she was to use this freedom to take her kids and come out of a horrible situation. Instead, she stayed and used the freedom of the Lord to make her husband pay. The sin of disobedience and the transference of the spirit of lust from her husband and his lovers caused her to fall into sin.

A few months after that she called me and told me she had a dream, where she had died in her sin and this big black demon came and grabbed her by the wrist to take her to hell. She said she fought him but he would not let go. She woke up scared to death. She told me that the demon that came to get my sister was real because he was the same demon who came to get her. She repented and believed God to deliver her. Sisters, having sex out of the will of God is no joke!

Remember R Kelly's song called "Your Body's Callin" A verse in the chorus says, "I hear you calling me." The calling he heard was from the realm of the spirit. It was stirring up his flesh to have sex outside of his marriage with young girls. Who was calling him? Spirits of lust was calling him. To be more exact the spirit of succubus. This spirit sexually arouses men in their sleep. The spirit of incubus sexually arouses women in their sleep. In the world, they call this a "wet dream." The lust of the flesh was ruling his life which caused him to write songs sexual in nature. As long as you live there will be a spirit ruling you. The question is which one will you let rule you, the spirit of God or of Satan.

I remember one time while having phone sex with a man me not even having to touch myself. It literally felt as if I was having sex with a man. I told this person how it felt like he was actually there. He took that as a compliment. Little did he or I know I was having sex with a spirit called incubus! I did not learn the truth until God introduced me to Kimberly

Daniels books. I went to God in prayer and did exactly what I suggested you do. Now I know what I am dealing with when the enemy tries to come back and attack me. I was asleep one night and dreamed that I was having sex with my husband. I looked under the cover and there was a big snakehead looking back at me. In my sleep, I rebuked him and pleaded the blood of Jesus against him. God allowed me to come out of my sleep speaking in tongues. I jumped out of bed and took authority over that demon, in the name of Jesus! I advise you to go purchase her books. She goes into more detail about this and other sexual sins. It will change your life.

While watching the movie "Ray" the Lord confirmed just how powerful sex can be. How linking your life with the wrong man can have devastating consequences. There is a scene where Ray was singing the song; "Night Time is the Right Time." While watching the song come alive on screen, I was shocked to find out the song was birthed out of an affair with one of his backup singers. Those of us who did not grow up in that era remember this song from the Cosby Show. It is one of the Cosby Show's most beloved episodes. The more I watched the movie the more my spirit was grieved. This woman was not a drunkard or drug abuser before she met Ray Charles. After sleeping with him, she became one. She opened a door in her life that would have major consequences. There was one scene in the movie where she begged him to shoot her up because she wanted a connection to him, even if it meant something as drastic as abusing drugs together. Their relationship was a toxic mess. The song "Hit the Road Jack" came out of their nasty break up after a night of sex and substance abuse. This woman later overdosed and left behind a child. The soul-tie was so strong that when he heard the news that she had died, he had to leave his son's birthday party because he was so distraught. His wife looked on in disbelief. So, if you think that only a physical connection takes place when you have sex with a man, you are sadly mistaken!

This movie reminded me of another movie called "Why Do Fools Fall in Love. This is the story about teen

72

idol Frankie Lymon, his sudden rise to fame and tragic fall in the music industry. He married three different women during his short life and when he died of an overdose, these women were left to duke it out over his estate. This movie grieved my spirit as well! Yet, after leaving "Ray" I was a little more informed about sex in the realm of the spirit and how music can be used as conduit to lure people into sin and they not even know it. I wonder how many people had affairs after listening to that song all night long in the club.

I had a family member who recently passed away. Years before her death the Lord had me to call her several times to tell her to stop doing what she was doing. God did not go into details and it was not any of my business. I have learned once God start having people call you to tell you to stop sinning, He has already talked to you several times, and you refused to listen. It is just a matter of time before He exposes you and then His judgment. The Lord started dealing with my husband about her and he called her a couple of times to minister to her. She did not receive the words of the Lord. One Thanksgiving we were having dinner at her sister's house. Her sister told me their mother would not attend Thanksgiving if my husband and I wanted to pray for her. I told her we would not pray for her and for them to come to dinner. When they arrived, we just said hello and left her alone in the living room. She was so ill! My husband called her a few more times after that only because God pressed upon his heart to do so. The word God gave was that her sickness was not just physical but spiritual. He told her she backed out on a promise she had made to God. If she would make true on that promise he would heal and restore her. She still did not receive the word of the Lord.

Her sister revealed to me that she was dating a man who was a convicted child molester. He had been in and out of jail for years. She had a daughter by this man. They even locked him up from her house one time because of an anonymous tip. She stayed in and out of the hospital and when I would speak to her sister she

would tell me they did not know what was wrong with
her. They kept claiming it was some "jail" disease
from her boyfriend. I did not believe it for one
second. I thought they knew the truth but was keeping
it a secret from me. I was in her neighborhood one day
and decided to drop in on her. What I saw broke my
heart. She looked like a ninety-year-old woman. I knew
I could not show any emotion because her mother was
looking to see if I was going to pass judgment. Until
the end, this family member major concern was about
this man even though he already had another
girlfriend. When he would come to see her, she would
still try to dress sexy for him. She would slip on a
teddy while wearing a Depend undergarment. Even in
this state, all she could think about was this man. He
rarely came to visit her or their daughter and when he
did visit, he acted as if he wanted to be nowhere near
her. I know this broke her heart! This family member
died leaving behind four children. On the day she
died, her mother told me she had AIDS and she asked
her not to tell anyone until after she passed away. I
was hurt but not surprised.

When her mother told me how she found her, half on
and half off the bed. I knew there was some type of
struggle in the realm of the spirit. Even her sister
shared with me how they would find her hiding behind
the bed and how she would call her mother's boyfriend
to come in her room to see if he saw what she saw in
her ceiling. He never saw anything but her behavior
scared him. In that moment, I thought about my sister
and her death. The sad thing about it is this man is
still sleeping around with other women.

I worked for a man who I later found out was a
homosexual. He was married to his wife for nineteen
years and she recently had a stroke. The next thing I
knew she left him and moved out of state. In the
meantime, he was living a homosexual lifestyle.
However, at the same time he was trying to convince
his wife to come back home. Finally, she decided to
come back and try to make the marriage work. When I
heard of this, I prayed that she would not come back
because I saw what he was doing at work. I saw

firsthand how he was telling her one thing over the phone and living something very different here. He would leave at lunch to have afternoon delights then come back as if he did nothing wrong. I knew he did because at times I could smell it on him. One day it smelled so bad I was sick to my stomach and it grieved my spirit! I was sick for the rest of the day until midnight that night. It was so bad I did not talk to my husband the whole ride home from work. I did not let my kids neither my husband touch me nor kiss me. I did not want to transfer what I felt unto them. I went straight to the shower and I stayed in there for the longest time. To let you know I was not crazy a few days later a co-worker came into our office (I shared an office with him) and said it stank. He said it smelled like someone's behind.

His wife came back and she looked horrible. She looked old and like she had been through hell. A friend and I prayed that she would not have another stroke or die because of his deceitfulness. We prayed God would have grace and mercy on her and expose his down low behavior. She lived with him for about a month but left after she found out by his friend (a co-worker) that he was still having homosexual relationships. She confronted him about it but he denied it. She found out the truth, left him and went back home.

If his sin grieved my spirit the way that it did then I know it grieves God spirit a billion times more when we sin. It is like dung in His nostrils!

I wrote you in my earlier letter that you should not make yourselves at home among the sexually promiscuous. I didn't mean that you should have nothing at all to do with outsiders of that sort. Or with crooks, whether blue or white-collar. Or with spiritual phonies, for that matter. You'd have to leave the world entirely to do that! But I am saying that you shouldn't act as if everything is just fine when a friend who claims to be a Christian is promiscuous or crooked, is flip with God or rude to friends, gets drunk or becomes greedy and predatory. You can't just go along with this, treating it as acceptable behavior. I'm not responsible for what the outsiders do, but don't we have some responsibility for those within our community of believers? God decides on the outsiders, but we need to decide when our brothers and sisters are out of line and, if necessary, clean house. 1 Corinthians 5:9-11 Message

I know it may not be cool to live holy anymore not even in the church. You do not hear holiness and righteous living preached in the pulpit these days. I am telling you that the best thing you can do is to live holy and to save yourself for marriage. A few minutes of pleasure is not worth physical death, spiritual death, emotional death, and loosing the blessing God have in store for you.

Chapter 7

PRAYER

Father, In your son Jesus name. I praise you because you are God. I glorify your name because you are just and pure in all your ways. I thank you for your sufficient grace. Let it cover me as I come before your throne today. Lord, I confess that I did things my way. I chose a man outside of your will for my life. I gave him parts of me only my "Adam" should have had. I confess that I have lived a life that was sexually impure and totally agianst your word. Lord, I repent and ask that you would forgive me of my sins. I do not want to continually give myself away in this manner. Father, I want you to break and destroy every soul-tie that has kept me in bondage to sexual sin. Give me the strength to cut off all ungodly relationships that hinders my walk with you. I ask you to renew my mind so that I will not make the same mistake again. I do not want to walk in a path that leads to destruction.

Holy Spirit, lead me and guide me in all truth. Create in me a clean heart and renew a right spirit within me. Give me the strength to live holy and to stay sexually pure until marriage.

I know if I seek you with my whole heart then I will find you. So, I come to You as the woman did with the issue of blood. I reach out today to touch the hem of your garment. Let me drink from Your water today that my thirst may finally be quenched. Lord, I ask that you restore me, give me a new hope and a purpose that I may serve you faithfully. Make me into the woman you destined for me to be. And when you are ready send me my "Adam" that I may be one with him. In your son Jesus name, Amen.

PART 2

HIM

Chapter 8

HE IS A UNBELIEVER

*I have a lot more to say about this, but it is hard to
get it across to you since you've picked up this bad
habit of not listening. By this time you ought to be
teachers yourselves, yet here I find you need someone
to sit down with you and go over the basics on God
again, starting from square one—baby's milk, when you
should have been on solid food long ago! Milk is for
beginners, inexperienced in God's ways; solid food is
for the mature, who have some practice in telling
right from wrong.*

Hebrew 5:11-14 Message

An unbeliever is anyone who has not confessed Jesus
Christ as their Lord and Savior and who does not live
and walk in the purposes of God daily. Involvement
with an unbeliever, makes you unequally yoked and out
of the will of God for your life.

*Stay away from people who are not followers of the
Lord! Can someone who is good get with someone who is
evil? Are light and darkness the same? Is Christ a
friend of Satan? Can people who follow the Lord have
anything in common with those who don't? 2Corinthians
6:14-15 CEV*

In this scripture, God clearly states that we have nothing in common with an unbeliever. So, why do we continue to become personally involved with one? Could it be the lack of knowing what God says about it? On the other hand, do we know what God says about it and are willfully disobedient to His word?

Do not be so deceived and misled! Evil companionships (communion, associations) corrupt and deprave good manners and morals and character. Awake [from your drunken stupor and return] to sober sense and your right minds, and sin no more. For some of you have not the knowledge of God [you are utterly and willfully and disgracefully ignorant, and continue to be so, lacking the sense of God's presence and all true knowledge of Him]. I say this to your shame. 1 Corinthians 15:33-34 AMP

The Old Testament tells the children of Israel not to yoke two different types of animals.

You shall not plow with an ox [a clean animal] and a donkey [unclean] together. Deut. 22:10 AMP

If you ever watched a western, you never saw a buggy attached to a horse and a cow. The buggy is always attached to two of the same kind of animals. To yoke two different kind of animals side by side with different heights, build, walk, and cause them to pull together is crazy. The people in the buggy will never get to their destination. The two animals will fight each other and one will tire and give in to the way the other wishes to go. The ride would be a ride from hell. The same applies to a believer and an unbeliever hooking up together. I do not care how strong you think you are you will be pulled away from God.

I knew a widow whom had been single for many years. Her daughter introduced her to a man she met in a car accident. They started to date and one day she went over his house and once there he went to dim the lights and turn on the radio to the slow jams. She told him she was not a loose woman. He backed off for a moment then moved in for the kill. Some heavy petting took place before she asked him to take her home. She shared with me her experience and I suggest she not put herself in a position where this could happen again. I asked her had she thought about seeing him during the day and out in public. If you do not put yourself in situations that could lead to sin that is half the battle. She agreed and tried this for a while. She even stopped seeing him for two weeks but said it was difficult to continue. I touched basis with her again to see how she was holding up. She told me she knew how to keep herself and that she had been doing it for years. I gently reminded her that the Holy Ghost had kept her. She blew me off and slept with this man. I guess his persistence paid off!

About a week later she gave him an ultimatum; marry me or else. He wanted to wait and not rush into anything. She persuaded him to honor her with marriage and her persistence paid off. They married a few days later. Later on, she told me if she were not afraid of burning in her flesh, she would divorce him. The man she married had a form of godliness. He was active in his church but had no personal relationship with God. Men who respect God are not going to do anything that will cause you or him to fall into sin!

King Jehoshaphat is a good example of a person being unequally yoked. Jehoshaphat was a king of Judah and he was a good king. He did not seek after or worship other gods but worshipped the true and living God. Jehoshaphat was a rich and honorable man but he made an alliance (hooked up) with Ahab (Jezebel's husband)." Ahab was the king of Israel and he was wicked. To seal their alliance Ahab gave his daughter Athaliah in marriage to King Jehoshaphat's son Jehoram. After some time Ahab persuaded Jehoshaphat to go with him to war against the Arameans to take back the city, Ramoth-Gilead. They were defeated and Jehoshaphat almost lost his life. King Ahab did lose his life. When Jehoshaphat returned to his house, the prophet Jehu confronted him and said, "Should you help the wicked and love those who hate the Lord and so bring wrath on yourself from the Lord"? His alliance with Ahab was judged as helping the wicked. We should walk away from all associations that would involve promoting wickedness.

Blessed is the man who does not walk in the counsel of the wicked, stand in the way of sinners, or sit in the seat of mockers. Psalm 1:1 NLT

Later Jehoshaphat makes another alliance with Ahab's son Ahaziah. The Bible says, "He acted wickedly in doing so." Jehoshaphat and Ahaziah built merchant ships in Ezion-Geber for trade with Tarshish. The ships were destroyed and Jehoshaphat suffered great financial loss. Nevertheless, it was in the marital alliance between his son Jehoram and Athaliah the greatest damage was done.

After Jehoshaphat's death Jehoram took over the kingdom. The Bible says, "He killed all his brothers, with the sword, and some of the rulers of Israel also." I read a biblical commentary on Jehoram's life and it said, "He walked in the way of the kings of Israel. Just as the house of Ahab did (for Ahab's daughter was his wife) and he did evil in the sight of the Lord. The political alliance of Jehoshaphat played a major part in the death of all his sons. After Jehoram's death his son Ahaziah ruled. After reigning for one year, he died in battle. His mother Athaliah (Ahab's daughter) seized power and had all the royal offspring of the house of Judah destroyed. After Jehoram and Athaliah's massacres, all that was left of Jehoshaphat's offspring was one great-grandchild. All of his other children, grandchildren, and great grandchildren were murdered. This story reveals alliances with wicked people are devastating (read 2 Chronicles chapters 17-20).

When you link with an unbelieving man, you will bring your God and he will bring his god to the marriage. Which god do you think you will follow? If you said yours, you are mistaken! The story of Jehoshaphat explains it all!

I want all of you to be free from worry. An unmarried man worries about how to please the Lord. But a married man has more worries. He must worry about the things of this world, because he wants to please his wife.

So he is pulled in two directions. Unmarried women and

women who have never been married worry only about pleasing the Lord, and they keep their bodies and minds pure. But a married woman worries about the things of this world, because she wants to please her husband. 1 Corinthians 7:32-34 NLT

This passage of scripture tells you that a married woman wants to please her man. Whether he be saved or unsaved. She will do whatever it takes to keep the peace and be pleasing to him even if this means compromising her beliefs to satisfy her husband. If you still do not believe read on.

King Solomon was obsessed with women. Pharaoh's daughter was only the first of the many foreign women he loved—Moabite, Ammonite, Edomite, Sidonian, and Hittite. He took them from the surrounding pagan nations of which GOD had clearly warned Israel, "You must not marry them; they'll seduce you into infatuations with their gods." Solomon fell in love with them anyway, refusing to give them up. He had seven hundred royal wives and three hundred concubines—a thousand women in all! And they did seduce him away from God. As Solomon grew older, his wives beguiled him with their alien gods and he became unfaithful—he didn't stay true to his GOD as his father David had done. Solomon took up with Ashtoreth, the whore goddess of the Sidonians, and Molech, the horrible god of the Ammonites. I Kings 11:1-5 Message

As I continued to read about King Solomon, I found this scripture. It reveals that Solomon knew what kind of wife he had married. This woman could not even stay in the royal house because of the presence of the Lord.

Solomon brought the daughter of Pharaoh out of the City of David into the house he had built for her, for he said, My wife shall not dwell in the house of David king of Israel, because the places are holy to which the ark of the Lord has come. II Chronicles 8:11 AMP

I had a friend who married an unsaved man. He would beat her up, belittle her in front of others, cuss her out, and cuss the God she served too. He cheated on her and brought home sexual diseases. He would not keep a job. He got another woman pregnant. He also treated their children bad. Her defense about his behavior was years ago the Lord told her that he was her husband. She was going to stand on this word no matter what. She believed this with her whole heart! She compromised with him all the time. She talked about the Lord and his goodness to others but no one receive what she said because they had seen her go through with him. The last time I spoke to her, it was not any better. Not every voice you hear is the voice of God! If Satan can transform himself into a being of light, he can also transform his voice.

These people are false apostles. They are deceitful workers who disguise themselves as apostles of Christ. But I am not surprised! Even Satan disguises himself as an angel of light. So it is no wonder that his servants also disguise themselves as servants of righteousness. In the end they will get the punishment their wicked deeds deserve. 2 Corinthians 11:13-15 NLT

The gatekeeper opens the gate for him, and the sheep recognize his voice and come to him. He calls his own sheep by name and leads them out. After he has gathered his own flock, he walks ahead of them, and they follow him because they know his voice. They won't follow a stranger; they will run from him because they don't know his voice." John 10:3-5

I had another friend who married an unsaved man after dating him for a few years. Before she married him, she called me and told me she was getting married. I asked her did she love him and she told me no. I asked her why marry him. She said she did not want their daughter growing up without a father in her life. Her other reason was she felt the Lord wanted her to make a decision, get married or stop shacking up. She also admitted that she was afraid to live alone. This was the start of a mess. Not only was he not born again, he had no work ethic. When he did work, she found the job for him. He would not keep the job for long. He always had some excuse for why he quit. This went on for years. He finally gave his life to Christ and served him for a few years. However, her patience was short by then and she did not want to go through the process of him renewing his mind. She had an affair because of this.

A former co-worker I knew married a religious man. She allowed him to be a stay-at-home dad while she worked for years. He was also on drugs and at times, he would steal her money, take her car over the weekend, and not return with it or even call. She would have to call someone to go take her to look for her car so she would have a way to get to work on Monday morning. After a while, she knew where to go to get her car and he would straggle home later that week. One time she was crying to me about his adulterous ways and I said, "You need to get out of this." She looked at me and said who will take care of the kids and me? I looked at her in utter disbelief that she would even ask me that question and said, "You will! You've been doing it all this time by yourself!" This man is still doing the same thing to this day.

In each of these cases, the women paid for their husband's clothes, shoes, food, video games, computers, music equipment, and cars. They gave them spending money, drug money, money to spend on their whores. Their husbands stayed at home and did not work. They had their "boys" and whores trampling through their house while they were at work. They were eating their food and running up their bills. After reading this do you believe that dating or marrying an unbeliever is what God wants for your life.

In three of the friend's case, they gave their men an ultimatum. Marry me or else! Ultimatums do not work! You force the man to make "your" choice, which is to marry you. Do you think he is going to walk away from the lap of luxury you provide for him? You provide computer equipment, music equipment, videos, video games, DVD's, clothes, free room and board, food, sex, money, and cars. What unsaved, unemployed, nowhere to live, busted and disgusted man would turn that down? None I can think of! This is not what the Father wants for you, nor is it His design for marriage.

Women, this is God's order for marriage.

- *He who finds a [true] wife finds a good thing and obtains favor from the Lord. Proverbs 18:22 AMP* Let him find you! If he is not a born-again believer who has a personal relationship with Christ, he is not the one! God is not going to send you an unbeliever for a husband. It goes against His word!

- *Then Adam said this [creature] is now bone of my bones and flesh of my flesh; she shall be called Woman, because she was taken out of a man. Therefore a man shall leave his father and his mother and shall become united and cleave to his wife, and they shall become one flesh. Genesis 2:23-24 AMP* The man is to ask for your hand in marriage! He is to buy the ring not you! I know of a woman who bought the ring and gave it to her man to propose to her. This behavior is desperate! This will turn a real man off!

- *Husbands, go all-out in your love for your wives, exactly as Christ did for the church-a love marked by giving, not getting. Christ's love makes the church whole. His words evoke her beauty. Everything he does and says is designed to bring the best out of her, dressing her in dazzling white silk, radiant with holiness. And that is how husbands ought to love their wives. They're really doing themselves a favor—since they're already "one" in marriage. Ephesians 5:25-28 Message* If you are not seeing any of this there is a problem. Your potential mate should respect and cherish you. He should never encourage or force you to do anything that will compromise your relationship with Jesus Christ.

- *But if anyone does not provide for his own, and especially for those of his household, he has denied the faith and is worse than an unbeliever. 1 Timothy 5:8 NASB* A husband will love and take care of his wife and kids. It does not matter if they are his natural children or step children! No real man of God is going to lay around all day at home while you are out making a living for the family.

I hope you have your paper or notepad near. I want you to write down your definition of an unbeliever. You might find that your definition differ from God's.

You might still be saying my man "know" God. Satan knows God but they are not friends. I knew God and believed in Him when I was a sinner but had not confessed Jesus as the Lord of my life. I did not have a personal relationship with Him. Let me explain it this way. One day I was on You Tube and saw where Oprah said there are many ways to God or whatever you choose to call Him. The Lord spoke to my spirit and said, "Theresa if you went to Oprah's condo or studio in Chicago would you be able to see her directly?" I told him no. I would have to go through the proper protocol to see her. He then asked me do I think I could go to her house in California and see her. I told Him no. They would probably arrest me if I tried to go near her gate. He then asked me could Gayle see her. I said sure, because they are friends and have been for a very long time. He then said, "If people who are not her friends have to go through the proper protocol to see her, shouldn't people who are not friends of mine have to go through my son Jesus to get to me. "Am I not worth much more respect," He asked me? I told Him yes and more!

Therefore, if your male friend is not tight with God like Oprah and Gayle are tight, then you need to keep it moving.

I Assure you, most solemnly I tell you, he who does not enter by the door into the sheepfold, but climbs up some other way (elsewhere, from some other quarter) is a thief and a robber. But he who enters by the door is the shepherd of the sheep. John 10:1-2 AMP

Chapter 9

HE IS MARRIED

"You shall not commit adultery. Exodus 20:14 CEV

God wants you to know there is nothing special about a woman who sleeps with a married man. For some strange reason the other woman always think, she is better especially in the looks and bedroom department. This thinking comes from Satan himself.

But, a man who commits adultery lacks judgment;
whoever does so destroy him.

Blows and disgrace are his lot,
and his shame will never be wiped away;
Proverbs 6:32-33 NIV

What the Lord is saying in these two verses is "You lack good sense"! You lack the ability to look at your situation and come to a sound conclusion that it is not going to work. He goes on to say that, you will destroy yourself and heartache and loss of respect will be your share from this mess. Adultery is a work of the flesh, *Galatians 5:19*. It is a selfish act. If you do not believe, look at King David's story.

King David committed adultery with Bathsheba, got her pregnant and had her husband killed in the line of

duty. King David went a whole year as if nothing was
wrong or nothing ever happened. He thought that he
could keep this hidden from God but God sent his
prophet Nathan to confront him about his sin. Praise
God David repented and confessed his sin to God (read
Psalm 51). Yet, there was still a price to pay. The
price David had to pay was the death of his son
conceived through adultery with Bathsheba. The sword
never left from his house. God brought calamity out of
David's own house on him by taking his wives and
giving them to one who was close to him. God let him
know the sin he committed was done in secret but what
God spoke about him would be done in daylight. Even in
this God was merciful. He allowed David to live!
Praise the Lord for that! *2 Samuel 11 & 12:1-24*

Some women may read the story of David and Bathsheba
and think it is romantic because of the lengths he
went through to have her. There is nothing romantic
about lust, adultery, and murder; it is sinful. All of
King David's actions were about what he wanted and
never about her. *He watched* her bathing naked, *he
lusted* after her, *he called* her to him, *he slept* with
her, *he got* her pregnant, and *he killed* her husband.
He did not think about how this would affect his
relationship with God. He did not care about whom
would hurt. He did not think about the price that he
would have to pay. Does this sound like love to you?

Another sad point is Bathsheba had no choice in the
matter. She was living in a time when women did not
have a voice and considered lower than a dog. What
could she do? How could she say no to the king? She
did not know if he would have her killed if she did.
What if she loved her husband and did not want to be
with King David? In today's society, women have a
choice whether they want to be with a married man or
not. God wants you to stop being silly and make the
right choice, the godly choice.

*Drink waters out of your own cistern [of a pure
marriage relationship], and fresh running waters out
of your own well. Should your offspring be dispersed
abroad as water brooks in the streets? [Confine*

yourself to your own wife] let your children be for
you alone, and not the children of strangers with you.
Let your fountain [of human life] be blessed [with the
rewards of fidelity], and rejoice in the wife of your
youth. Let her be as the loving hind and pleasant doe
[tender, gentle, attractive]--let her bosom satisfy
you at all times, and always be transported with
delight in her love. Why should you, my son, be
infatuated with a loose woman, embrace the bosom of an
outsider, and go astray? Proverbs 5:15-20 Amplified

After my older sister divorced, she dated married
and involved men. One particular man she dated, the
relationship lasted about 10 years. "Brian" would
always come over our house to see my sister and they
would sit on the couch and have open displays of
affection in front of everyone. It did not even matter
if a child was in the room. Eventually they would head
to her bedroom to take care of business. There was
nothing but sex between them anyway. He rarely took
her anywhere. Nobody liked him and we came not to like
her as well. She would talk about his wife like a dog.
She never stopped to think all the information she was
getting about his wife was from him. You cannot
believe what a married man tells you about his wife
and their life together. He will tell you what you
want to hear to keep having sex with you. Toward the
end of their ten years together, my sister became
sick. One day she went into a diabetic coma while I
was driving her to the hospital. Before she passed
out, she gave her life to Christ. She was in a coma
for three days and on the third day, she woke up. She
came home from the hospital and when he found out she
was home he came over. Four months later, my sister
was dead.

The night she died, I had a dream that my sister was
sitting on a witness stand. She looked beautiful. God
was sitting on the throne as judge. Jesus and I were
standing next to one another. I began to beg my sister
to accept Jesus as Lord of her life. She refused my
words as Christ himself stood there with me. My sister
crossed her arms over her chest like a rebellious

child and suddenly her eyes burst into flames. I woke
out of my sleep praying in tongues and jumped out of
bed. While I was asking the Lord why he allowed me see
this I saw a big black demon come through the wall
were my sister was sleeping on the couch and grab her
by the wrist. He was big and I knew he was the demon
who took people straight to hell. He yanked her up off
the couch. She fought him but nothing stopped him. I
asked the Lord let me go help her and he told me do
not open the door and stay in the room. I thought
about my niece who was out there with her and I
thanked God my children decided not to sleep with my
sister this particular night. I was still praying in
tongues and I heard my nephew come out of his room and
go to the bathroom then back into his room. I thought
it was strange that he did not go to the kitchen as he
always did at night. The demon pulled her through the
wall like a kite blown by the wind. I said to God,
"How am I going to go to sleep after seeing all this"?
He then said to me, "Sit down," I sat. "Lie down," I
laid down. "Close your eyes and go to sleep." I did. I
woke up the next morning and went to the bathroom. I
brushed my teeth and as I was washing my face, I heard
my niece yell, "Theresa my mom is unresponsive, help!"
I went into the living room and I started yelling for
my nephew to help us. He pulled her off the couch
while I dialed 911. As I was talking to the operator
my nephew looked at me and said there is no need for
the ambulance to come she is dead and has been for a
few hours, call the morgue.

At the wake, her lovers were there and she left
behind parting words for each of them. She wanted them
read at the service. After my oldest niece read the
first paragraph, the preacher asked her to take her
seat. The Pastor did not know my sister he was my
mother's pastor. Nevertheless, he preached that day!
My family, her friends, and lovers sat stiff neck
refusing the offer of salvation. The air was so thick
in the church that day you could cut it with a knife!
I cried as I sat next to my girlfriend. My tears were
not because of her death but because I knew, where she
went. A couple of months after the funeral I shared

with my sisters what God had showed me the night of our sister's death. They did not believe me. They believed that she went to heaven and did not want to hear anything else about it.

A year passed and her daughter confided in me that after her mom came home from the hospital from being in a coma she told her how Jesus had appeared at her bedside. He told her that if she would give up "Brian" and serve Him he would heal her from diabetes and give her another chance. I knew this was true because in 1992 the Lord told me the same about healing her, if she would give up her sinful ways. Obviously, she accepted the Lord's offer because she came out of the coma. After hearing this, I heard the Lord say, "Theresa, I gave her every opportunity as you asked." I remember being thankful that day for Him answering my prayer. It gave me peace even though she bust hell wide open. One time I even thought it would have been better if she had died the day she went into the diabetic coma. At least she would be in heaven right now.

Brian is still alive today. He got a divorce from his wife whom he cheated on with my sister. He probably does not even realized how blessed he is to have another chance to get right with God and accept Jesus as his Lord and savior. I pray that he do.

This happened to an unbeliever. Imagine what will happen to you who believe.

"And a servant who knows what the master wants, but isn't prepared and doesn't carry out those instructions, will be severely punished. But someone who does not know, and then does something wrong, will be punished only lightly. When someone has been given much, much will be required in return; and when someone has been entrusted with much, even more will be required. Luke 12:47-49 NLT

Is this what you want for your life? Are you willing to pay this price? The Lord is not playing with us. He is tired of the mess we are making of our lives messing around with married men. He is tired of us acting silly. He is tired of us sleeping with the enemy and then crying to him when we have not seen nor heard from the joker in five days. He is tired of us seeking for a word from Him giving permission to stay with a married man! It is not going to happen so get over it! Stop receiving and believing so called prophecies telling you "so-and-so" are your husband when he is married. This goes against the word of God!

A close friend of my husband and I called us for advice. She said that she went to her spiritual mother's church one Sunday to visit. After service, her spiritual mother told her about the service held last Sunday. They had a guess preacher and he prophesied to a male member of the church that his wife is in this church. The pastor gave this man a description of the "wife." There was a woman there who fit the description and the man asked the guest preacher about her. He said she was not the one but another woman fits the description. Now fast-forward to the Sunday my friend arrived at her spiritual mother's church. The man who received the prophecy saw my friend who arrived with a brother in Christ. He asked the pastor (her spiritual mother) if my friend was married to this man and the pastor said no. My friend said that she had seen this man a few times when she visited before but never found him attractive. After hearing what took place last Sunday, she suddenly found him to be attractive. She wanted to know what she should do. My husband reminded her that she is married (not to the brother in Christ she came to church with) even though she is separated. He told her she should not be thinking about being with someone else. She should focus on receiving healing so she can be whole. My husband told her this is not of God because God is not going to tell you some other man is your husband when you are already married. He told her there is a deceiving spirit working and it wants to keep her in bondage. After getting off the phone with her we asked ourselves, "Why didn't her spiritual mother tell this man she was married?" This made us wonder about the motive of her spiritual mother's heart towards her. What happened to the standard of holiness in this case?

I know of a sister in Christ who had a baby with a married man twenty years ago. I will call this sister "Angie." During the years they have had an on and off relationship. It was on when she was not married and off when she was. The wife knew Angie was the other woman and that she had a child by her husband. They have even talked a few times. His wife was a Christian as well. About a year ago, he decided to get a divorce from his wife because Angie finally put her foot down and told him she would not deal with him any longer. About the same time, the Lord began to deal with me about Angie being sick in her body over the years. The Lord told me that her association with this married man opened the door to demonic attacks on her body. This is why she has had the sickness and surgeries she has had over the years. The Lord also told me that when she marries him she would regret it for the rest of her life. I asked her aunt to relay this message to her and her Aunt's comment was "Angie's going to do what she wants to do." Angie and this man were planning to marry that summer.

A few months ago, I saw Angie at a revival and she was worse. She could not even move her neck. She could only look straightforward and if she did turn to the side, she had to turn her whole body to talk or look at you. Her movements were stiff like a robot. Her aunt recently told me that Angie did marry this man. It was sad to hear. She never told Angie what I said. She told me she was offended by what I said. She wanted to know how could I make that statement and not even know him. I told her I was only telling you what God revealed to me. She said she understand that now. Does Angie think any good fruit is going to come out of this union? Does she think she will not receive some works of adultery in their union together? No child of God is immune from His correction!

A girlfriend of mine is going through a separation from her husband. She was taking it hard and wanted him to pay for his indiscretion. God rebuked her while driving one day. He told her to stop acting as if she had never did anything wrong. He asked her did she remember the affair she had with a married man in 1996. She told him yes but that was different, he and his wife were separated. God told her it was not. Then he reminded her about the pregnancy during the affair. He told her she is just reaping the harvest from the seed of adultery she had sown. She asked God did he make her husband have an affair on her. He told her no, his own lust drew him away. No one can sow a seed whether good or bad and not reap a harvest. The Lord told her to be thankful that she has believers around her to pray her through this difficult time. His wife did not have anyone to pray her through and she is still stuck in 1996. My friend received what the Lord said and told me she was going to find a way to apologize to this woman. Can you imagine the healing that will take place in the both of their lives if she follows through with the apology?

Opening the door of adultery will bring all manner of sickness, disease, and evil to the willing participant. Even Brian went through major sickness and had to have several operations. He is still having major operations to this day. Now you see why God calls us silly women. I pray these stories have opened your eyes to the truth of God's word and that you will come out of adultery and fornication and be holy as the Lord God is holy.

If you want to come out here is what you do.

- *Make it right with God!* Repent and confess your sins to Him. This brings you back into fellowship with God and allows you to be covered under the blood of Jesus.

- *Call it off!* Get in touch with your lover by text, phone, fax, or e-mail and break it off. What should I say you might ask? The God of Abraham, Isaac and Jacob told you to come out of sin. There is no further explanation! God does not care if he has been separated from his wife from one minute to several years. If he does not have a certificate of divorce, he is still married in the eyes of God. If you are in a relationship with him, you are an adulterer.

- *Pack up his belongings!* If you were shacking up, place his belongings where he can retrieve them without interacting with you. Do not keep any of his belongings or nothing he brought you. Let me tell you why. I broke it off with this person and gave him back his stuff but kept the letters he wrote me in a box in the top of my closet. One Sunday at church, the pastor prophesied about someone having a box of love letters in the top of their closet right now. He said this was the last obstacle holding this person up from being free. I knew he was talking to me. I went home, took that box out of the top of my closet, tore every one of those letters up, and threw them and the box in the trash outside! I was set free that day because I obeyed the Lord. On the other hand, if you are living with him leave and find you another place to go without leaving him a forwarding address. You can go to the post office and put in a change of address. Take only what belongs to you. Do not act petty over rings, clothes, TV's, and furniture. This stuff is replaceable. God is able to get you new stuff!

- *Do Not Be Afraid!* During this time, you will see a different side of your lover. It makes no difference if he is a "saved" or unsaved he will be angry and will act mean towards you but do not worry. I have learned if you obey God, he will protect you! Please obey the Holy Spirit! I broke up with a person because the Lord told me to and I told him what God said. At first, he was cool about it because he knew I had a relationship with the Lord. The next day he called me and told me he was going to stalk me. He told me that if he could not have me nobody would. I was concerned about this but one day as I was waiting for my sister to open her door (I was picking up my kids). I felt the presence of the Lord and I heard the Lord say, "He will not stalk you." I was praying aloud as my sister opened the door and she began to pray with me. He did not stalk me either! He went on about his business and left me alone. Praise God! If he is a nut job, seek counsel from someone you trust and let the Lord lead you from there. The Lord does not care how crazy this man may be acting. His craziness does not stand a chance against the Blood of Jesus Christ!

- *Live Holy before God!* Make up in your mind that you want to live a clean life before God. Stop fornicating and wait on God! When you are frustrated, tell God. When you are horny pray and ask the Holy Spirit to help you through it. When I was going through this, I had older women of God in my life who prayed me through. They were not afraid to be real with me or share their stories with me but they never let me forget holiness was the standard. I thank the Lord for that. If possible, surround yourself with real women of God who will pray for you and understand what you are going through. Most of all their desire for you must be the will of God for your life. If you do not have support, ask God to lead you to a church of his choosing. While you are waiting for this to happen, thank him and know that, he has you in the palm of his hand. He did it for me and he will do it for you. One time I visited this church and my son started crying during altar call. The pastor asked me to hush my baby or leave the sanctuary. In that instant I heard the Lord say, "Leave and never return to this church again." I left the sanctuary and when I got outside I told the Lord I'm not going to church again unless he find me a church to go to. About a year later, a coworker of mine introduced me to a Pastor friend of hers who became my Pastor and spiritual mother. God placed me where he wanted me and I learned how to pray, worship and live holy under this woman of God. Remember the pastor who asked me to leave his church? One day I saw him on the evening news. He was in jail for molesting little boys. God cares about every detail of your life! Trust Him! God is good I tell you!

- *Stay in the word of God!* Read your bible daily and pray without ceasing. Read scriptures on adultery, fornication, and forgiveness. Speak aloud to the devil because he will come at you with all types of stuff to get you to go back. When he realizes you are standing your ground against him he will try to condemn you about what you did. Use your sword (the word) and whip his tail with it! I do not care if you have to speak the word to him one hundred times a day. He will not give up without a fight but God has guaranteed you the victory! Ask the Lord to lead you to books that will help you through this. Here are some books that helped me. Breaking Unhealthy Soul Ties by Bill Banks; Seductions Exposed by Dr. Gary L. Greenwald; What to Do Until Love Finds You and Secrets of an Irresistible Woman by Michelle McKinney Hammond; Woman Love Your Body by Apostle Louis S. Greenup.

Chapter 10

YOUR CHILDREN DO NOT LIKE HIM

I remember as a little girl being afraid of my cousin's husband. Every time we went over their house, I would stick close to my sister or try to stay hidden because I did not want him to see me. He would find me anyway and chase me. I would run like the wind from him! He gave me the creeps! I do not know what it was about him but I knew something was not right. Have you ever experienced that as a child?

A child has a way of seeing through people in a way we adults cannot or choose not to see. My niece told me her daughter does not like her cousin. She said every time she sees him she grabs me, hides her face and starts screaming. She tells me she does not want to see his face. I told my niece her daughter sees something in him that you do not. I told her not to force her to go or be around him if she feels like that. When a child tells you they do not like someone or shows this behavior when they are around someone, as a parent you need to listen and take heed. I have seen this happen repeatedly with parents not listening to what their kids have to say.

As a parent, we should listen to our children and hear them out. God is not limited in the ways He work or in whom He uses. If He can use a donkey to get Balaam's attention, He surely can use a child. Speaking of animals remember when the Tsunami hit. The newspapers reported the animals ran for higher ground before the Tsunami hit. I also read where some tourists were on an elephant ride tour before it hit and when the elephants felt a forewarning, they took off for higher ground. The guides tried to restrain them and keep them on the trail but it did not work. If an elephant has sense enough to take heed and run away from danger, what is wrong with us? When your child tells you, they do not like your male friend you need to ask your child why without being intimidating. This is not some thirty-year-old child living in your house that do not have a life and do not want you to have one either! This child needs to feel safe and protected. If a child cannot feel safe in their own home, where can they feel safe? What affects you affects your child. Whatever situation you find yourself in with a man your child will be a part of as well.

When I was a girl, I would go to visit my sister and her family at their home. They had a neighbor who had three girls. I was close in age to the middle daughter. We became friends and I would go over their house and at times spend the night. They had a stepfather who they did not like. He did not work and he always gave them grief. They were on punishment all the time. I could not understand it because they rarely came outside to get in any trouble. When I would get a chance to talk to them, they would tell me their mom put them on punishment because he said they did not clean up their room. I remember one time I went to see her and she was upset. I asked her why she was upset, she told me she asked her mother for a new pair of shoes, and she said no. She showed me her old pair of shoes and the sole was detached. It was wintertime and they had to wear those Catholic uniforms with the socks up to their knees. She went on to tell me her stepfather told her (while her mom was present) he did not think she needed a new pair of shoes. He told her this lame story about when he was a boy he had to wear shoes worse than that to school. Her mother did not get her any shoes either. I felt sad for her. I wanted to buy her a pair of shoes so bad. She saved up her lunch money and allowance so she could buy herself a pair of shoes. I am glad to say she graduated from college and is doing well. The last time I spoke to her, she ran a home for abused and troubled children.

Ladies, if you are dating or married to a man that tells you your children do not need this or that, you need to get rid of him. If he has something negative to say every time you do something for your children he is not the one! This man is selfish, jealous and insecure! I bet he never have a problem when you cater to his needs! If he is always punishing your children for no legitimate reason and always speaking negative about your babies, you need to kick him to the curb. He will be abusive to your children on the sly! Nothing you do will please him. He will always find a problem in how you raise your children, how you run your home, the way you dress and how you live your life. Yet, he never contributes anything positive, meaningful or fruitful to you and your children lives. Let us be honest for a moment. You are not staying with this man for the money he contributes to your home because he contributes little to none. The sex is not what is keeping you in the relationship. Because when you see him being mean to your children you do not want him to touch you. You are afraid to be alone and you need to suck it up, kick his behind out, apologize to you children and move on with your life. Wait on the Lord to bring you your "Adam" and stop being so desperate for a man!

A family friend was having a difficult time with her mother during her last year of high school. She called that year the worst of her life. Her mother met, moved in and married a man who had nothing going for himself. Soon the atmosphere began to change in the house and arguments ensued. Her mother deliberately picked arguments with her, called the police on her several times in an attempt to put her out of the house. This man only instigated the arguments and this made the child not like him. Her mother took her bedroom door of the hinges. When I heard this, I prayed because this is a door opener for her to be abused by this man. Her mother refused to give her a ride to work. She would make this child walk back and forth from work on a darkened highway. She lived in a rural area and anyone could have kidnapped her. She would call my daughter and talk with her during these walks back and forth from work to home. The mother brought this man a car when that car could have gone to her daughter. This man even went so far as to accuse this child of having sex in their bed when her mother found a piece of hair in their bed that was not hers. She went off on her daughter instead of being repulsed by his accusation. This man should have been kicked to the curb with a steel-toe boot!

This child is not a bad child. She made great grades, went to school every day, held a part-time job, was not on drugs nor having sex. Yet, this was not enough for her mother. She would not even help her get into college at first. This child was so upset that she called us crying. My daughter and I prayed that God would change her mother heart and show her the error of her ways. I am glad to announce that God did it and she is in college. I spoke to her mother during one of their rough patches and she could not give me a valid reason for why she was upset with this child. She even admitted that she had a good daughter. What was the problem then? Her husband was the problem. The spirit of division and confusion operating in him caused a rift between her and her daughter. Men, who are confident in themselves, secure in their relationship and who love their woman will not come in between her and her children. A real man understands that you hold many roles as a woman. Your role as a mother is just as important as your role of being his girlfriend or wife. He should respect that and do his best to encourage peace between you and your children. You should run away from a man who always finds fault with your children!

A friend of mine invited me to go to church with her and her family. After church, her husband was hungry

and wanted to go to McDonalds. The kids got excited
when they heard McDonalds and asked could they get
something to eat. Their father turned around, yelled
no and told them to stop being so greedy. My friend
calmed the children and told them she would fix them
something to eat at home. He then turns around and
asks me did I want something to eat. I told him no
thank you. I would not dare eat in those children
faces knowing they were hungry. This was not the only
time this was done in my presence and my answer was
always no. It was not as if they did not have the
money. How can a father eat in front of his children
and not offer them something to eat as well. Every
month without fail, he would give his list of what he
wanted and he would get it! He got everything he
wanted from computers, video games, CD's, and even
pets. The children as always received only the bare
necessities, if that.

We would go to the store with our children and she
would happen to see one of her children chewing gum.
She would ask them where they got the gum from and
after much prodding; they would tell her they got it
off the ground. She would ask for the gum, spank them,
and tell them how nasty it was to do that. I would ask
her to let me buy them some gum and she would tell me
no. She said they were just being greedy. These
children were not greedy they were hungry! She spent
most days running after her husband, trying to keep up
with his whereabouts that the children did not eat
most days until nine at night. I have even caught them
searching through the trash looking for food. This was
not necessary since she received enough money every
month from the state to provide for them.

One time I stayed with them while going through my
divorce having no place to live. She said I could
sleep in the boy's bedroom. I went to lie on their bed
and it was a box spring! I was shocked and upset that
these boys were sleeping in this type of condition. I
went to the store and brought some foam padding to
make it bearable for my daughter and me to sleep on.
One day my daughter and I were in the boys room
sleeping and suddenly I heard her husband scream,

"Look what you did." He said this repeatedly. I did not know what was going on. I was afraid to come out of the room. He repeatedly reminded his son that it was all his fault and the dog would be put to sleep. Meanwhile, I was trying to figure out what had happened. I was scared to leave the room because I did not know if the dog was running loose or tied up. This dog was a Rottweiler and I had already experienced waking up to him staring me in my face one morning. I could hear him on the phone screaming and whining to my friend about the dog being put down. He was not concerned about his son's welfare. He did not call the ambulance or take his son to the hospital. We only lived five minutes from the hospital. He waited until she drove home from work and they both took him to the hospital. When they came back, she told me that her son had agitated the dog and that is what she told the doctors to keep the authorities from coming to get the dog. Their son needed stitches on his cheek and of course, they did not get rid of the dog. The next day the Lord revealed to me what had happened. His father cooked a big meat bone for the dog. The son being hungry went to take some meat off the bone while the dog was eating and the dog bit him acting territorially.

While staying with them she would come to my room and say her husband wanted to know if I wanted to watch television with them. I would decline. She never asked herself so I thought this was weird. Besides, my mother taught me not to hang around other women men without them being present and to limit my presence when they are with their man. After this, I decided to leave their house before she left for work or when she was leaving for work. I would stay out all day and come home when she came home or near the time, she would be home. This was so I would not have to be in the house with him by myself for long. Even though our children where there I did not feel comfortable being there when she was not. When I did not have anywhere to go during the day, I would stay in the room with my luggage against the door. There was no lock on the door so if he or the dog would try to come in, the movement of the luggage would awaken me. I kept snacks and drinks in my room so that I would not have to go to the kitchen. Her children would come to my room and I would share with them what I had. I knew they were hungry and he was not going to feed them. Soon after I heard the Lord say, "You need to leave ASAP. He is going to try something with you." The Lord told me to call my mother-in-law and ask could I move back in with her. I did and she let my daughter and me move in the next day. I cannot even begin to tell you how good God has been to me!

A few years later while talking to her on the phone. I just got tired of listening to her justify his horrible behavior. I shared my perspective about what I saw as an outsider looking in. She tried to cut me off but I refused to back down. I reminded her about the abuse and mistreatment of her children, as well as herself. She was in total denial. I told her she was going to look up and find that her children did not want to be bothered with her. This will be due to the years of abuse at the hands of their father. I asked her what answer she would give for not coming to their rescue. I told her they will never want to come home for the holidays because of this and she will pretend as if she does not know why they are acting this way. The conversation got so intense that it ended on a bad note and we did not speak to each other for a while. Yet, I never regretted sharing my feelings with her about the way her husband treated her and his own seed! One day the Lord showed me a crack in a foundation. I asked Him what this meant. He told me "There is a crack in their foundation and their house is going to fall."

We spoke again a few years after this and she shared with me how one of her children had gone wayward. The details of the situation were devastating and she came across as if she had given up on her child. She was pretending as if she did not know why her child was behaving in this manner. She said doctors diagnosed this child as bi-polar and she received it. I asked her not to receive their words but she said she was tired of this child and put her in the Lord's hands.

Yet, she still defended her husband after all the years of abuse; she fought for him like a crazy person and never gave up on him. Is not her child worth that same type of effort? I was heartbroken after listening to her! My heart was so heavy that I felt never to touch the situation again.

My husband and I were introduced to two sisters who unbeknown to us married abusive, unsaved men. We did not know that these sisters allowed their husbands to physically and verbally abuse their children. The oldest sister had a beautiful daughter with a bubbly personality. Yet, behind that personality laid a pain we knew nothing about. One day her daughter came over our house to visit with my daughter. They were about to go out to eat with a friend but before they left my husband wanted to pray for them. While my husband was praying I happened to look at this young lady and the Lord showed me a spirit of suicide on her. When I told her what I saw she began to cry. While we continued to pray for her I saw her mother walking on her tiptoes as if she was walking on eggshells. Then I heard the Lord say, "Reign of Terror." While I continued to pray the Lord showed me that the reign of terror was her father and that he had been so for many years. I asked this young lady to call her mother and I told her what God told me. There was a silence over the phone as God continued to reveal that her husband was a tyrant. God showed me that she could not pray aloud or do praise and worship in her own home! The silence turned to muffled cries over the phone while her daughter sat on the steps weeping. This man made their lives a living hell! The mother admitted to the abuse but said it was not as bad as it once was. She said she stopped him from beating the children a while ago. Yet, the verbal abuse and hatred toward God continued in the home. God told me to tell her that her husband's reign of terror was over. Either he could get it right or God would move him.

The youngest sister had this same type of abuse going on in her home as well. She asked my husband and I could we pray for her, the family and bless her home. My husband asked her did she check with her husband first because we did not want to overstep our boundaries. She said it would not be a problem. We arrived at her house and were greeted by a beautiful woman (we were meeting for the first time) with two equally handsome young boys. She introduced her oldest son to us first. When I heard him speak I heard the Lord say, "Professor". I told his mother and grandmother what I heard the Lord say. They both said it was not the first time someone had told them that concerning him. We went into their family room to pray and God revealed some really deep stuff through my husband. When she revealed to us that her husband was beating this little boy with two grown man belts put together my heart sank. She admitted that she has stopped her husband from beating him at times because he was going overboard. I looked her in her eyes and told her she must stop this abuse from happening to her son. I felt as if she knew how to deal with her husband in such a way that he would leave their son alone and I told her this. We did not get a chance to bless the house but we prayed for them days afterward.

One night around midnight as I was worshiping God the Lord dropped this child's name in my spirit. I saw his father standing in the door way of his bedroom debating whether or not he should wake him up and beat him. I asked the Lord to send the most fearsome angel to protect him. I asked God to let his father see this angel just like Balaam saw the angel with his sword drawn. I asked God to let that angel put the fear of God in his heart so that he would not put his hands on this child again. While praying in the spirit the Lord showed me that His hand is upon this boy's life. God reminded me when I first met him and when he opened up his mouth to speak, I heard the word professor. God showed me that this child is going to be a professor. He will be one who professes (to declare or admit openly or freely) the word of God. He will not be some community college professor, but one who will be very well known. He will be most sought after.

The Lord went on to say that because of the call on his life, his mother must get her mind off of herself. Her past is over and she need to stop trying to recapture it. She must take her focus off of her husband, his money, the house and his hefty insurance policy. She must stop looking to her husband as her way out. Her husband is not the way out her son is and she must put the focus on him. He must be nurtured, protected and she must lead him in order for him to reach his destiny. She is the gatekeeper and if she covers and protects him now is the same way he will cover and protect her later in life. God then showed me LeBron James mother. He said even as a sinner she saw the potential in her son to be great basketball player. She covered, protected and directed him and now has reaped the benefits of his success, though she is acting real foolish now. The Lord went on to reveal that the reason why her husband treats the second son a little better is because his mother favors him. Despite this, she is to treat both sons with love, care, concern and without favoritism. The second son will glean (pick up) what you teach the oldest son. I relayed this message to her later that evening. I pray she is taking heed to God's warning!

The oldest sister on the other hand is trying to do damage control from the years of abuse. We have ministered to her daughter several times afterward and she shared with us that she does not think she will ever be able to forgive her father. And once she graduates from college she will never return home for a visit.

Fathers, do not provoke or irritate or fret your children [do not be hard on them or harass them], lest they become discouraged and sullen and morose and feel inferior and frustrated. [Do not break their spirit.]
Colossians 3:21 AMP

The Lord explained to me that we are gatekeepers over our children lives. What we allow to come in and go out of our lives will affect our children. If we give the enemy access through our gate, our children will be destroyed but if we keep our gate closed to the enemy, our children will be fine. In that moment, I understand how important my life was. That being a mother was special and God chose me to shepherd two wonderful children! The Lord told me to call a family member and tell her what He said. About a month later, I had a dream and emailed her this note when I got to work.

I dreamed Shawntise, "Brianna," and I were hanging out together. We stopped by your house because Brianna forgot something. I went to look in your room and a man was lying on the floor. I only saw him from the chest down at first. He had all tan on. He realized I was in the room and he stood straight up without bending. When I looked him in the face, he was black and shriveled like an old dried up raisin. I knew that it was "Mark" and uneasiness came over me and I left the room. When I reached Shawntise and Brianna, they knew something was wrong. Brianna asked me what was wrong. I told her nothing. She asked me did Mark scare me and I said come on lets go. Being Brianna, she went upstairs to confront him about it. Shawntise and I waited and we heard nothing and I knew he had did something wrong to her. I told Shawntise to stay put and I raced up the stairs to get Brianna. While I was running up the stairs, I felt he had killed her. I woke up from the dream and I felt a demonic presence that took me a while to shake.

I went to the bathroom and the Lord began to talk to me about the dream. He brought to my memory the movie Fright Night. How this character Charlie knew that his next-door neighbor was a vampire. He read all he could on the subject of vampires. He put garlic and crosses all around his room. He even nailed the window shut. He thought he was safe until his mother called him downstairs to meet a guest. When Charlie walked down the steps, he saw the back of the chair the guest was sitting in and when the guest stood up, it was his next-door neighbor the vampire. In turn, the vampire smugly said to Charlie, "Your mother welcomed me into your home anytime I want." Charlie was devastated because he remembered reading that a vampire can only come into your home if you or someone invites him. There his mother stood smiling, deceived by this neighbor's good looks and charm. She was blind to what his true nature was.

Then the Lord told me that if you invite this man into your home it would be the worst mistake of your life. He will turn your home, your children, and your life upside down. For years, you ran out on your husband and had no care, but this man will run out on you thrice the amount you ran out on your husband and you will do or say nothing about it. He will beat you and your children into submission. He will break you and your pride like a man breaks in a horse. They beat the horse until its spirit is broken. When a man's spirit is broken, he will do anything his master wants because there is no more hope. The Lord went on to reveal that you laugh at your sister, brother and others lives, but you are in no better shape than they are! You are blind just like they are! Your sin is just as offensive as theirs is! Do you think there is no price to pay for your adultery, fornication, and pride? Do you think that God does not see your sin? He does and your stench has come before Him as dung!

Are you willing to pay the price with Brianna's death? If the answer is yes, then that is exactly what you will get, say's the Lord God Almighty! God is always just in His actions and His word never lies! Just because you do not believe, it does not mean it is not true! For God knows the heart of man, that it is defile and wicked. You know this man only by the flesh and what he want you to see about him. God know his heart! She replied with, "I'm numb. I've been asking for help and for vision and this is what I was waiting for, now I don't know how to continue." I shared with her what she need to do and left it at that. Guess what, she is still with him and her children do not care for him either. My husband and I even mediated between her and her children about this man. Instantly, she turned defensive, became stiff neck, and would not listen to a word we said. I have watched this behavior over again with women. They always justify their man's behavior. They defend him no matter what he does. Their man can do no wrong. Yet, God is still faithful! He knew I was concerned for Brianna. Therefore, He told me not to worry and that He has her and her brothers. Since that time, I have had a peace about it. People do not even realize that they and their children are alive today because somebody prayed and is standing in the gap for them.

A year later, she revealed to me that she let him read the email I sent her that day. She said he did not speak for about three days. When he finally did speak, he asked her, "Does your aunt really think I would do something like that?" I told her it is not what I think it is what God knows. She explained to him my "spiritual life" and that I talk to her in this way sometimes. Many times, we think we have escaped God's word because it did not happen when He spoke it. That is not the case. God's word always manifests, maybe not in our timing but in His timing, it will speak and not lie.

Recently, she shared with me that she wants to get married to him but he does not want to marry her. He had many excuses from her color choices to where they should get married. His other excuse was the way she disciplined her children. In addition, her housekeeping skills were in question. He told her when these issues are resolved then he will think about marrying her. This hurt her feelings. She proceeded to defend the discipline of her children and house cleaning habits to me. There was no need because I know her. I know how she disciplines her children and what type of house she keeps. Let me just say, that he is lying and even if she did all the things he requested, he will still find an excuse not to marry her. He is running game and what God said about him is true. It is foolish to ignore such a dire warning from God! She needs to move on with her life before it is too late!

If you think this, only happen to women you are wrong. A male family member married a mean and nasty woman. Before this woman even came into his life, the Lord had me to tell him that he had to be careful of the type of woman he has around his son. The Lord said that his son was special to him and he did not want him mistreated or abused. Even after this woman came into his life, the Lord had me call him again after a Thanksgiving incident concerning this woman and his son to warn him again. He told me that he knew this woman did not have any motherly instincts because she did not demonstrate them with her own children but he was sure he could teach her how to love her children. His son even had to stay with his grandmother for a while because he did not like this woman and she did not want him living with them. What got me is that it was ok for her children to live at his house but not his son! Even after his son came to live with them, she would make his biological mother visit him out on the front porch and her children's father could come in their house and visit his children. They are still together and she is still mean and surly! I even heard his son call her mom. It sent shivers down my spine. He recently lost custody of his son because of his wife and her children's abuse toward him. The son told the judge about how his stepmother and her children were mean to him. The judge gave custody to his biological mother.

This is how our children are being destroyed! Listen, if you being a parent of some type of sound mind stand back, watch and allow your child be abused by another parent (biological or step-parent) or even a boyfriend or girlfriend and do not step in to stop the abuse, **then you are no better than they are!** There is a big difference between discipline and abuse. Discipline is training that produces moral, mental, physical and I will even add spiritual improvement. Abuse on the other hand tear down, hurt and injure people physically, mentally, emotionally and spiritually. Children look to us for safety and protection and if a child does not feel safe in their own home or cannot find refuge in you, where can they find safety? What will be your excuse later in life when your grown child asks, "Why didn't you protect or stand up for me?" What account will you give God concerning your indifference toward the abuse? PLEASE

STOP PROTECTING AND DEFENDING THE ABUSER. PROTECT AND
DEFEND THE ABUSED!

Molestation is a fact! A few years ago, I had a
friend and her family come to visit me. She told me a
girlfriend of hers and her daughter would be coming
along. When her girlfriend daughter walked through the
door, I saw sexual abuse on her. She was around seven
at the time. Then this man walked through the door
behind them and I felt he was the one doing it. I
pulled my friend aside and asked her who was he. She
told me it was her friend husband and the little
girl's father. I told her that this man was sexually
abusing his daughter. She did not believe me. She
looked at me as if I was crazy. A few years later, she
revealed to me that this man was in jail for molesting
that little girl (his daughter) and a friend of hers.
She said when I pulled her aside that day and asked
her who he was; she did not like the tone in which I
asked the question. She said she now realize that when
I speak in that tone I am speaking by the power of the
Holy Ghost.

When I was married to my first husband, we lived
with his family for a bit. His sister and her
boyfriend lived in the same house as well. They had
two daughters. He stayed at home and took care of them
while she worked. He would keep the girls locked up in
the room with him all day. My daughter would want to
play with them and he would tell her they could not
come out of the room right now. He would not even let
them sit with their grandmother at times. His behavior
disturbed me and I would keep an eye on my daughter at
all times. When he would say she could come in his
room and play with them, I would not let her go. I
would only let her go when their mother was home. One
day I told my husband, his mother and his older sister
that I felt he was molesting his daughters and they
needed to do something about it. They just looked at
me as if I grew another head right in front of them.
Later that night, my husband told me he believed me
but his sister would deny it and take the side of her
boyfriend. He said he did not feel like arguing with
her. As the girls grew older, he would sleep with the

girls in their bedroom with the door closed. What man leaves the bed of his girlfriend to sleep with their daughters? I never understood why she allowed it! I moved out when they were ten and eleven but I knew in my heart this abuse would still go on. My daughter would tell me that they said they hated him and would be glad when he would stay away from home for several days. They are young women now and both of them are lesbians. I can understand the root of why they have decided to live this life. Their mother is upset that they have chosen to live this lifestyle and is acting as if she does not know why this may have occurred. A year ago, their father passed away. At my daughters graduation party I could see my ex sister-in-law was still grieving over him at the mention of his name. This saddened me because she wasted so many years on a man who brought nothing worthwhile to her life except for their two wonderful daughters. I am tired of seeing this happen to the women that I love and care about!

Sexual abuse encounters are horrific especially if the perpetrator was your father or a close family member. These people are supposed to protect you from horrible acts such as this. Sexual abuse encounters can open the door for the spirit of homosexuality to enter in a person's life. It also opens doors of lust, perversion, fornication and promiscuity. Spirits of shame and disgrace are major players the enemy uses to plague your soul. The enemy will try to tell you it was your fault and that you deserved it. That is a lie from the pit of hell! No child or adult deserve to be taken advantage of! If you have been sexually abused or encountered any other type of abuse, please tell someone! Do not walk around with this pain inside of you as if nothing has happened. Share your story with someone you trust and/or seek counseling.

Abuse is a fact. When I was a kid we use to have this saying, "Sticks and stones can break my bones but words will never hurt me." That is a lie! The bible says the power of life and death lies in the tongue. People use their tongue to damage children every day. I use to visit my aunt and her husband for two weeks during the summer. This woman put my mother down at every turn and made it a point to belittle me. She never cussed at me nor raised her voice but her words hurt just the same. I struggled with this all of my life until God began to bring healing unto my soul. In 2005, the Lord had a friend of mine call me and tell me that I should write a letter to my aunt to release the hurt I had been carrying. This is what I wrote.

I pray this letter finds you well today! I am writing because I want to express a certain heaviness that I have carried with me for thirty-five years. I have learned that words carry the power to heal or destroy. Most often we remember the words that destroy, especially if very few healing words were spoke to us in our life. Coming to your home in the summer months were not pleasant for me, due to never having been away from home. Yet, they were made even more unbearable because of the destructive words that were spoken to me. In your view, they may have not been harsh, but to a little girl they were. To tell me I would never succeed in the workforce because no employer would want an overweight woman representing his or her company was hurtful. To tell me I would probably never marry because no man wanted a fat woman as a wife was just heartbreaking. To make things worse you criticized every little thing I did or ate while at your house. To be told that I could not go to the beach with Jasmine and Tyrone because I was fat and that I would be an embarrassment to them was just cruel. To watch the look on their faces when you told them I could not go and to see William walk away with them was devastating. I knew that day it was not them who did not want me to go, it was you. You were ashamed of me. For whatever reason, I do not know. Your words and actions caused me to seek love and acceptance from people I had no business being with. I have struggled all these years trying to prove your words wrong. No matter the great successes I have had in my life, I could not enjoy them because they never seem to be able to knock down the destructiveness of your words. What you said and did was wrong and no excuses can be made for it. I remember a picture that was taken at your house; in that picture was myself, William and another little boy. As I took the photo in, I realized that I was not fat. I was a normal size little girl, but it did not register within me at that time. I was never what you said I was. I only became what you said I was because I did not know nor understand the truth of who I really was. The saddest thing yet is to see the destructive power of your words trickle down to "Stacey" and "Kim". At "Uncle James's" house, I observed Stacey and Kim together as you were introducing them to the family. Kim was self-confident with her head held high. While taking in the comments of how she looked just like my sister. Stacey had no self-confidence. She never made eye contact with anyone and walked with her head down. When I saw this, I knew that she had been touched by the destructiveness of your words. I wanted to take her in my arms and love her. I wanted her to experience the power of Jesus healing me at that season of my life. No child should ever have to endure hurtful and harmful words, especially from people who are suppose to love them.

If you never tell a person what they are doing or have done is wrong, then how will they know it. This revelation gives you the choice to change and do right or continue to do wrong. In the end, the choice is yours, but this takes the burden off my shoulders whether you acknowledge your wrongdoing or not. Like the woman with the issue of blood, who suffered many things because of her condition, said to herself, "If I can just touch the hem of his garment I shall be made whole." The Lord has made me whole and now I can move on with the rest of my life!

Be careful of what you allow people to speak over you and your children! The enemy will use people to speak curses over your life. The devil is so on his game that he will try to use the same curse in another generation. My nephew, his wife and her two kids stayed with us for a few months. She boasted on her daughter because she was tall and skinny had a light complexion and green eyes. His wife took it upon herself to tell my daughter that she was fat and that she needed to lose weight. She did this in front of me. Instantly, I heard the lord say, deal with that spirit. I knew exactly what the Lord meant. I pulled her aside and told her my story about what my aunt did to me. I let know that I was not going to allow that spirit to use her to do to my daughter what it had done to me. In addition, I would be out of line if I told her daughter she was anorexic looking. There she stood taken aback but she knew I was not playing. My daughter was not fat at all but the devil wanted to sow a seed of self-body hatred into her life. I had a long conversation with my daughter and I shared my story with her. To this day, you cannot tell her she is not beautiful. I praise God for his love and divine intervention.

I cannot tell you how many stories I have heard of children being molested and/or abused by their mother's boyfriends, baby-sitters, and relatives. I was molested several times as a child. My babysitter's son molested me while in her care. I must have been three or four. My mom had to work and at that age how could I explain to her what happened to me. I did not even know what had happened to me. The sexual abuse continued from time to time. I can remember a family member and my sister's boyfriend putting a bb gun to my head while having me touch this family member penis. All this occurred while they were getting high. How would they have explained this to the police if they would have accidently shot me?

Stop leaving your children unattended for long periods of time home alone. Especially, with men you barely know. All kinds of things can happen to them. Children are a gift from God and you will have to give an account one day for how you took care of them.

Fathers, do not irritate and provoke your children to anger [do not exasperate them to resentment], but rear them [tenderly] in the training and discipline and the counsel and admonition of the Lord. Ephesians 6:4 AMP

Chapter 11

HOW IT WORKS

It all started out as a word spoken or an action
taken against you. Something transpired maybe once,
for some repeatedly. You were hurt and because no one
seemed to care or because they just did not know how
to care, your hurt turned into anger. The anger
simmered into a boil over the years because there was
no one who understood your pain. In the deepest
recesses of your mind you thought you were to blame.
Words so sharp, actions so evil could make anyone go
insane. All is hidden and no one has talked, so you
have kept it all inside. Smiling as if all is well,
"that's a good girl," they said. You searched for a
salve to ease your pain; liquor perhaps will dull this
stain. What stain is that you say? The stain life has
left in the mind of someone's regret. Maybe the salve
of sex will erase the stain. This time I will do it
for me not because it was forced on me. That did not
work either. It only increased the need to be bitter
forever more. I can do no worse; let us try crack the
optimum choice. Lord, I made a mistake. I did not know
it could take me to this place.

Deceptive and cunning is what it is, a device
masterminded in Satan's liar. I have worked on it from

the start. Very smart isn't it? I start young you see. My rule is give them a salve to ease the pain. Broken families are my delight. One parent is all you need in these times. The slogan is "quality not quantity." Yeah, I made that one up also. I pray on those that do not know or reject God. They are easy for the picking. Do not get me wrong; I am no respecter of persons. I seek out Jesus pleasers as well. They just take a little more work though. Overall, I am an equal opportunity destroyer. Easy targets you are. You do not pay attention to those who hurt especially children. You are too busy with your boyfriends and /or girlfriends. Sex is the name of the game these days. It occupies the majority of your time. You can thank my lust demon for that one. You people are so self-centered. All you think about is your looks. Who would have thought that big boobs would be the craze? Pride and selfishness deserves all the applause. Fear is a on the rise. I am not surprised. I use that one a lot. You would be amazed at all the phobias I have created. I have crippled thousands with fear. It is my way of keeping you from living. I will do anything to keep you from your destiny and fear happens to work with some of you. Let me not forget about a drug for every problem and/or mood. A major devastation isn't it. I knew it would be. I needed some way to control you since I cannot be in two places at one time. This way I will know where to find you when I have to run off and do more hurt. Poverty is a big one I might add, since you are only home three to four hours in a day. I truly understand your plight. You have to make a living don't you. Meanwhile, I have the privilege of watching your kids. Win, win situation isn't it? It definitely works for me. I have countless other devices that I could mention that would make your heart fail but I hear "Despair" calling me from across town.

God gave me this in 2001

Chapter 12

HE IS A MOMMA'S BOY

This has to be a serious issue for the Lord to tell me to put this chapter in the book. Therefore, here we go. A momma's boy is *a grown male (saved or unsaved) who allows or desires his mother to control most aspects or decisions of his life for him.* How can a man be the head of a family when he cannot make one decision without running it past his mother first? Even as a child, Jesus was about his father's business.

And when Jesus was twelve years old, they all went there as usual for the celebration. After Passover his parents left, but they did not know that Jesus had stayed on in the city. They thought he was traveling with some other people and they went a whole day before they started looking for him. When they could not find him with their relatives and friends, they went back to Jerusalem and started looking for him there.

Three days later they found Jesus sitting in the temple, listening to the teachers and asking them questions. Everyone who heard him was surprised at how much he knew and at the answers he gave.

When his parents found him, they were amazed. His mother said, "Son, why have you done this to us? Your father and I have been very worried, and we have been searching for you!"

Jesus answered, "Why did you have to look for me? Didn't you know that I would be in my Father's house?" But they did not understand what he meant. Jesus went back to Nazareth with his parents and obeyed them. His mother kept on thinking about all that had happened.
Luke 2:42-51 CEV

Now being a child, he had to obey his parents but when it came time for his ministry to begin, he did not ask his mother's permission before going off to do the will of the Father. He just did it.

Just then his mother and brothers showed up. Standing outside, they relayed a message that they wanted a word with him. He was surrounded by the crowd when he was given the message, "Your mother and brothers and sisters are outside looking for you."

Jesus responded, "Who do you think are my mother and brothers?" Looking around, taking in everyone seated around him, he said, "Right here, right in front of you—my mother and my brothers. Obedience is thicker than blood. The person who obeys God's will is my brother and sister and mother."Mark3:30-35 Message

Mary did not step in the way of the will of God being done in his life. After Jesus had disappeared at age twelve, she prayed about it and I know she got an answer from heaven. "How do you know, you may ask?" Because she did not act like a fool when Jesus left for ministry nor was she acting all crazy when they handed him over to Pontius Pilate. Believe me it pained her to no end but she had a revelation from God. A revelation from God is the only way she could face and endure an unjust and tragic situation and come out of it not hating God or losing her mind. The problem with most mothers is they do not know how to put their nurturing instincts aside.

"But at the beginning of creation God 'made them male and female.'For this reason a man will leave his father and mother and be united to his wife, and the

two will become one flesh. 'So they are no longer two,
but one. Therefore what God has joined together, let
man not separate." Mark 10:6-9 NIV

When a man comes of age and decides to take a wife a
mother has to respect that. A mother has the liberty
to ask questions and express her feelings or concerns
on the pending marriage. If her son's mind is made up
her next step should be to show unconditional love and
pray. If she has laid a strong foundation (the word
of God, wisdom and discipline) for her son to stand
upon then she will not have to worry about his choice
for a wife. He has already been equipped to make a
sound decision, not just concerning a wife but also
for every other thing in life. Now, if his foundation
has been established on depending on his mother for
everything then he will. This includes all other
aspects of his life as well. If his mother has a
controlling spirit on top of it then his bride to be
is in major trouble.

There was a young woman whom I knew who was blamed
for everything that happened in her marriage. Her
mother-in-law never had a nice thing to say about her.
One moment her breath was stinking, the next moment
she did not know how to satisfy her son in bed. I
could go on all day. I listened to this for years
until she and her husband along with my husband and I
started hanging out together. One day we suggested
that we should all get together and talk about what
was going on with them. This came after an intense
argument between his mother, him and his wife at
dinner. We met over his mother's house to mediate
between them. His mother and a family friend were
there when this took place. The three of them sat
together, his wife sat alone, and my husband and I sat
on the couch. His mother, a family friend and her
husband spoke their peace without interruption. His
wife spoke last in a calm nonthreatening voice. She
said something they did not agree with and like snakes
moving in unison they rose out of their seat ready to
strike her. I could not believe what I was seeing! I
mean their bodies literally moved like a cobra ready
to strike! I jumped off the couch pleading the blood

of Jesus against those python spirits operating in them! The family friend got very upset, which was normal. Even when we would have prayer, she prayed angry. She told me I was nothing but trouble and every time I came around, I stirred up confusion. I told her she was the one who keeps up confusion. I turned to my husband and told him lets go.

A few years after this the Lord would bring his mother to my spirit and He would say, "Eli." I read the story of Eli again and prayed for her. He continued telling me this on and off for over a year. Her son also received several warnings about his lifestyle from different men and women of God. He would not listen. A few years later I heard the tragic news that he went to prison for a lengthy amount of time.

When I was a child, I spoke like a child, I thought like a child, I reasoned like a child. When I became a man, I gave up childish ways. 1 Corinthians 13:11 ESV

Here are some signs to look for concerning a momma's boy.

- A man who cannot make decisions for himself and has to have his mother's approval no matter what.

- A man who needs to talk to or see his mother on a daily basis and most likely more than once a day.

- A man who need his mother's permission to date or marry. There is nothing wrong with a man who wants his mother's approval concerning this big step. Harmony between the mother and his woman is essential, but wanting her permission is another thing altogether.

- A man who has to be manipulated to marry you has no backbone. If you had to stoop to this level for him to marry you, you have very low self-esteem.

- A man who has to sneak and date or marry you after his mother disapproves of you. You now have to pretend you two are not dating or married for weeks until he can find the "right time" to tell her.

- A man who responds to or races over to his mother's house every time she calls.

- A man who puts your plans on hold when his mother calls with other ideas.

- A man who allows his mother to disrespect you around him and others.

- You are blamed for everything wrong in the marriage and he can do no wrong in his mother's eyes.

Need I say more? If you are dating and find yourself in a situation like this one you need to exit stage right ASAP! Why would you want to compete with his mother for the rest of your married life? If he is not ready to let go of the breast then you cannot make him. Do not waste your time move on! If you are already married to a man like this, it has to be frustrating as all get out! On the other hand, maybe you have grown accustomed to this situation. Either way prayer or counseling is needed to make a wise decision on how to handle this.

Chapter 13

YOU ACT LIKE HIS MOTHER

In relationships today, many women find themselves being a mother rather than a wife to their mate. This is due to a spirit called Arrested Development. This spirit causes the development of a man or woman to stop prematurely. This can take place through some type of rejection, abandonment and/or trauma early in a man's life. It can also happen when his parents do not discipline him and have not ministered to his emotional, mental and spiritual needs for whatever reason. He will mature physically but spiritually, mentally and emotionally he will not. If your man grew up in a home where he never observed his parents go to work then most likely he will not feel a desire to work. If he never learned to clean up behind himself or bathe on a regular basis then he will take this behavior into adulthood. Maybe he grew up in a home where he saw his father be emotionally detached from his mother. Then he will exhibit this same behavior in his relationships and marriage. For him this is normal behavior because this is how he was raised. However, for you it may not be.

The spirit of arrested development can bring out a negative reaction in women as well. Have you ever asked your man to do something once and it takes him a week or more to do it? After a while you will nag (annoy by continual scolding, faultfinding, complaining and urging) him. When that does not work, the spirit of contention (fusing, yelling, screaming and arguing) is used to get your point across. Once you are tired of contending with him the spirit of frustration, (a deep chronic sense or state of insecurity and dissatisfaction arising from unresolved problems or unfulfilled needs) seals the deal. Months or years of this have left many women frustrated, tired and ready to give up on the relationship. This behavior has also lead to infidelity, separation and/or divorce in your relationships.

The bible says that the enemy comes to steal, kill and destroy. Satan loves it when parents are slack in doing the job assigned by God. Any door that is left opened for the enemy to attack a child's life he will come through. He loves it when men are not in their rightful place in the family unit. He loves it even the more when the father is absent from the household, whether it be body, soul and/or spirit. Therefore, women are left holding the bag and find themselves trying to raise a grown man.

Eli was a man who took his responsibility as a father and a priest lightly. His sons were scoundrels and had no respect for the Lord. They did detestable things concerning the sacrifices brought to the house of the Lord. Eli knew all of this but took it as a light matter. He did as many parents are doing now; he acted as his children's friend rather than their father.

Now Eli was very old, but he was aware of what his sons were doing to the people of Israel. He knew, for instance, that his sons were seducing the young women who assisted at the entrance of the Tabernacle. Eli said to them, "I have been hearing reports from all the people about the wicked things you are doing. Why do you keep sinning? You must stop, my sons! The reports I hear among the LORD's people are not good. If someone sins against another person, God can mediate for the guilty party. But if someone sins against the LORD, who can intercede?" But Eli's sons wouldn't listen to their father, for the LORD was already planning to put them to death. 1 Samuel 2:22-25 NLT

Because Eli refused to take heed to God's warnings, He sent a righteous man to give him this word.

So why do you scorn my sacrifices and offerings? Why do you give your sons more honor than you give me—for you and they have become fat from the best offerings of my people Israel! "Therefore, the LORD, the God of Israel, says: I promised that your branch of the tribe of Levi would always be my priests. But I will honor those who honor me, and I will despise those who think lightly of me. The time is coming when I will put an end to your family, so it will no longer serve as my priests. All the members of your family will die before their time. None will reach old age. You will watch with envy as I pour out prosperity on the people of Israel. But no members of your family will ever live out their days. Those who survive will live in sadness and grief, and their children will die a violent death. And to prove that what I have said will come true, I will cause your two sons, Hophni and Phinehas, to die on the same day! 1 Samuel 2:29-34 NLT

God spoke the last warning through Samuel.

Then the LORD said to Samuel, "I am about to do a shocking thing in Israel. I am going to carry out all my threats against Eli and his family, from beginning to end. I have warned him that judgment is coming upon his family forever, because his sons are blaspheming God and he hasn't disciplined them. So I have vowed that the sins of Eli and his sons will never be forgiven by sacrifices or offerings." So Samuel told Eli everything; he didn't hold anything back. "It is the LORD's will," Eli replied. "Let him do what he thinks best." 1 Samuel 3:12-14; 18 NLT

Eli's nonchalant attitude about God's judgment was the same type of attitude he exhibited in raising his sons. He honored his children more than he honored God and a terrible price was paid. God cursed his future generations due to his funky attitude. This is so sad. He could have raised sons that any woman would have been proud to have and priests that honored God in every area of their lives. This is what has happened to our men and what is happening to the young men coming up today. Listen, parenting has a lot to do with repeating the same things over again until the child get it. I think the frustration comes in for the parent when they feel like the child is not listening due to their facial expressions. We cannot be afraid of the looks on our children's faces and/or fear them not liking us anymore. Do not pay any attention to their faces!

> Train children to live the right way,
> and when they are old, they will not stray from
> it. Proverbs 22:6 NCV

I had a phone conversation with a friend who told me every job her husband has had is because she got it for him. She would call the company, set up the interview and her husband would go in and get the job. Every car he has ever had was because she brought it for him. For the most part everything he has ever owned since they have been together she has brought it. I told her she acts like his mother. She said she feels like it. After years of trying to teach him how to be a man, she is now living alone. A weight has been lifted and she is enjoying being single. This behavior can also affect a couple's sex life. What woman wants to sleep with a man whom acts like a child?

Ahab was another man in the bible who acted like a child. He ran to his wife to fix every problem that arose in his life. She loved it because she was wicked and a control freak. She did not know her place either in the marriage. She wore the pants in that relationship and she made that clear with her threats and murder committed against an innocent man. Real women want to feel protected and taken care of by their man. I know I do! This quality is sexy to a woman. When we know our men can take care of us and protect us this allows us to be free. We do not want to make all of the decisions. We were not created to be the head of the home but we can step up and lead if necessary like the Prophetess Deborah, read Judges Chapter 4 and 5.

I watched a reality show were this young medical student met a young man who was an artist. They dated for a while long distance and then she agreed to move in with him. They had problems like any other couple but he was not good with his finances. One day she went to visit her folks back home and when she came back from that trip, he told her he had not renewed the lease on their apartment. He said he thought it would be best if they would move in with his parents while he got his finances in order. She was upset! She told him no way. She did not want to live with his parents, so she left him. She accepted a job in another state to finish her medical residency. I was so proud of her. It was not that she did not love him but she loved herself more. That is our problem; we do not love ourselves enough!

A woman once told me that a good woman could make a bad man good. I had never seen that happen with the good women I knew so I disagreed. She could not give me any examples so I left it alone. Later the Lord ministered to me about our conversation. This woman grew up in a different generation. Her generation's mind set was to stand by your man. This is what they believe a good woman does. I believe a good woman can make a good man better. Yet, it is not our job to raise a grown man. The problem is that we do not believe that God can bring us a good man. We look at the men today and feel hopeless. We think we have to settle for whatever man comes along. This is not true. We box ourselves into thinking that our choices of men are only limited to whatever city or state we live in. We need to think cross-country or overseas. God is not limited in how He will bring your "Adam" to you. In addition, if women would just raise their standard then this will cause men to come up one or more levels in manhood. Men enjoy the chase. If you set the standard of no sex before marriage and stick to it, it will weed out the counterfeits. The man who honors your standard will do everything in his power to honor you and make you his wife.

If you are with a man who refuses to grow up and take responsibility for his life, then you need to move on. You trying to raise him again will only stop him from taking action on his own. As long as you are there to do it for him, he has a reason not to.

Here are some red flags you should not overlook.

- He is childish.

- He is lazy and takes no initiative.
- He has no goals of his own.
- He can't make sound choices or decisions on his own
- He has no job or cannot keep a job (not because of the recession).
- He stays at home and plays video games all day.
- You pay for everything all the time (dates out, rent, bills, groceries, etc).
- You have to remind him to do the simplest things such as bathe, brush his teeth, put on clean clothes. Only children need this kind of reminding.
- You call to wake him up every morning to convince him why he needs to get up and go to work.
- You are applying for jobs on his behalf.
- You brought him everything he owns even down to his underwear.
- You brought him every vehicle he drives.

- He cannot even plan a date or romantic evening without your input.

- He is insecure. He always has to have his boys around or someone to go with him.

Chapter 14

HE IS ABUSIVE

At eighteen, I met a young man at a neighborhood pool who physically abused me. He was controlling and jealous. He did not want anyone to talk to me not even my family. The first time he hit me was because I did not want to sit at his feet and watch a movie. I wanted to sit on the couch next to him. When I got up to go to the kitchen I felt this breeze behind me and the next thing I knew I had been body slammed to the floor. He was over top of me telling me never to turn my back on him again. I told him I was going to get something to drink from the kitchen. He asked me to forgive him and I did. The abuse continued and with the abuse came great fear. Any little thing would tick him off so, I would think about what I was going to say to him before I said it aloud. I would not miss a call because if I did I would incur his wrath. It was a rough time for me. The last and final straw for me was when we were about to go out and I had walked to my car to check the oil. I had asked him to fill a jug I had with water. Before I knew it, he had grabbed me around the neck and slammed me against the car. My feet were off the ground. I was a thick girl so for him to do that I knew he was either possessed or crazy! He told me never to talk to him like that again. He let me go and I looked up and saw the neighborhood kids were watching in amazement and smiling. I was so embarrassed. I went in the house to fill the jug with water and came back out to leave. Once on the road I decided to stay silent to keep the peace. He kept trying to get me to talk to him but I refused because I knew it was going to turn into a bad argument. Moreover, I did not want to be arguing while driving. I turned on the radio and he said you are going to listen to me. He grabbed the steering wheel and swerved us into oncoming traffic. The road we were on is a major road and usually there would be traffic coming. We hit the meridian strip before stopping. My first thought was I could have killed a car full of children. I started screaming at him, I told him we could have killed somebody. I asked him why he would do that. He yelled, "You would not listen to me." I backed the car off the meridian strip and pulled in a strip mall parking lot to get myself together. I got out of the car to look at the damage and began talking to God in my mind.

A young man pulled in front of my car and got out to ask me was I all right. I told him yes. He said he saw what happened and would be glad to take me home. Before I could answer, my boyfriend started talking trash to him while he was standing behind me. The young man told him to shut up and mind his business. He told my boyfriend he was not talking to him and called him a punk. He told him I saw what you did and you say one more thing I will take my pistol and bust a cap in you. My boyfriend was still talking trash while standing behind me. I told the young man I would be all right. He asked me was I sure and I told him yes. He told me I did not have to be afraid, he knew how to handle him. I told him again that I would be ok. I did not go with the young man because I looked in his eyes and I saw he was serious about shooting my boyfriend. I had lived in the hood long enough to know when a man is not playing games. In addition, I did not want this man to go to jail over him. I reassured him that I would be ok. I got in my car along with my boyfriend and drove back home. Because of the accident, a hole was in my radiator. I had to wait until my mother got home to use her car.

While waiting he begged and pleaded for my forgiveness but I refused to talk to him. Once my mom came home, I asked my niece to ride with me to take him home. I did not want to go alone. The whole way taking him home, he screamed, cried and stumped his feet like a baby having a tantrum. I ignored him and when we arrived at his house, he asked me was I going to call him when I got home. I told him yes. I convinced him to get out of the car but he continued talking to me from the rolled down window on the passenger side. When he backed up from the car enough for me to roll up the window, I put the car in reverse, and he went to punch the window out. I stepped on the gas and he started screaming that I ran over his feet. I kept going and never looked back. My niece laughed her head off. She said it took everything for her not to laugh when he was stomping and screaming like a baby. He continued to call after that but I never answered the phone. I had my family tell him I was not home when he called. After about a month, he got a clue and left me alone. God was merciful to me, a sinner. I made up my mind that day I would never stay with someone who is abusive to me. My niece and nephew told me about his behavior towards them when they were around us, years later. I did not notice it. They said every time they came around he would tell them to go away or get lost. I asked them why they did not tell me. They said they tried. We told you we did not like him. I apologized to them. I told them that while in the pool that day something told me to leave him alone and a bad feeling came over me. I ignored it and suffered.

I had a friend from high school who suffered major abuse. Our last year of high school she became pregnant and left before graduation. Years later, I got back in contact with her and she shared her story with me. She told me how she slept in the hospital waiting rooms at night (acting as a patient) because she did not have a place to live. Her baby's father would take their child and go over his girlfriend house to sleep at night and then bring the baby back to her in the morning. He would viciously beat her. She said one time she yelled at him and he punched her in the face as he would punch a man. One time he beat her in their front yard, ripped her clothes off and left her naked for the neighbors to see. That is devastating! She is still with him.

I remember one time my niece called me upset and wanted to come over my house. I asked her what was wrong. She told me that my sister's boyfriend had just chocked her brother. My other nephew stepped in but could not get my sister's boyfriend off him. Therefore, my niece went to her room and got her friend gun. She came downstairs, put the gun to his head, and told him he has to the count of three to let her brother go or she would blow his brains out. He let go before the count of three. Meanwhile, my sister is hollering at her asking her where she got the gun. She demanded that she give her the gun but my niece refused. She never addressed her boyfriend who was choking her own son to death. Her boyfriend was always verbally abusive when drunk. I even remember them telling me he spit in her face one time. Nobody deserves that treatment!

A few years later God gave me a word for her. He told me to tell her that He wanted to open doors for her to teach children. He said she would make a major impact on their lives. She was not to worry about her grandchildren because He was going to take care of them. He also wanted to bless her with a man who she could live the rest of her days with. God told me to tell her to get rid of her boyfriend whom she had been with for close to thirty years. If she did this things would manifest just as He said it would. She told me she could not put her boyfriend out after all these years. She was worried about what would happen to him. Sad to say she did not do it. She is raising her grandchildren along with helping to take care of him. He is sick because of many years of drinking and he refuses to stop drinking. An added load to the burden she is already carrying.

I watched an episode of a reality show where a young woman went to hang out at her friend's house. Her boyfriend called asking questions. After hanging up with him she told the women that she had to leave. She tiptoed out of that house to her car as if he was outside waiting for her. You could tell she was scared. I know she went through hell when she got home. I told my daughter this young woman's boyfriend is abusive to her. I know that behavior when I see it.

I use to attend a woman's group when I was a babe in Christ where we were free to discuss issues that mattered to women. Every Friday different women would attend and this particular night a woman who had an abusive husband attended. The meetings took place in the clubroom of the prayer leader's mother apartment building. The woman lived in this same building so her husband knew where she was. Her little boys would come downstairs from time to time during the meeting and peep through the glass. After two hours, he came down and looked through the glass. We prayed for her and asked God to touch his heart. He came back a few more times before opening the door to tell her she needs to come home. She did not want to leave because God was ministering to her, but my spiritual mom suggested she leave so he would not act out. She was a social worker who met and married this man late in life and had children with him. She said she regretted marrying and having children so late because now she did not have the patience to deal with it. She did not have to go into details because we saw what she had to deal with. After she left we interceded on her behalf. I have found abusive men to be cowards with low self-esteem. They prey on the weak and helpless. This makes them feel powerful. Their main weapon is fear and intimidation, which they use to control you. They want you to dedicate your whole life to them. They require you to cut off everyone around you. They do not want you talking on the phone to other people. Nor can anyone visit you. This is so that their voice will be the only voice you hear. They always have to know where you are going or where you have been. They want to control every aspect of your life. From what you eat and drink even to the clothes you wear. They are selfish and they give to you when it benefits them. You cannot even speak freely without fear of their wrath. You will think this is love or even cute at first but it will eventually turn into bondage.

Abuse is never acceptable no matter who is doing the abusing. I do not care how many times he apologizes after he hits you. God did not create you to be a man's punching bag! Neither was you created to be verbally, mentally, or sexually abused! If you are in an abusive relationship, you need to leave ASAP! You must be careful how you go about leaving especially if you have children. Every woman's case is different so I advise you to let the Holy Spirit led you in your exit.

Chapter 15

HE IS IN JAIL

A former co-worker introuduced me to her mother-in-law who was a Pastor. This woman became a spiritual mom to me. She was one of the women who taught me how to live holy. She and her husband had several sons. All whom they raised in the Lord. I was introduced to her son "Terrence" in jail and after a few phone calls we agreed to meet. My co-worker(his sister-in-law) and I went to go visit him. He was what I had expected and more. He was handsome and built like a mack truck. We continued to communicate by phone and mail. I visited when I could since he was far away. I sent him money when I could and encouraged him in any way possible. We talked about the Lord and he told me that my life was a life of prayer and fasting. He said there was no other life for me. He made God a promise that if he saw where he was going to mistreat me he would walk away. I started this letter writing campain to get him released from jail. It worked along with his family support, prayer and fasting. Before he came home I was looking at television one night and saw this video by a country singer called "I've Have the Best Intentions." It was about this husband who went to jail and left his family behind. He wrote to his wife that he had the best intentions concering her. I took

that as a sign. Right before he came home the Lord
said to me, "I did not call you to play the whore." I
told the Lord alright and went about my business.
About two months later Terrence came home and a few
days later we slept together. We fell asleep and I had
a horrible nightmare.

A demon was leaning against his brother's car. The
demon spoke to me and told me he had been assigned to
Terrence since birth. He said he would come in my
house and get him but he could not. He said I had too
many angels camped around my building so he could not
enter. He also said he could not enter Terrence
mother's home because she had angels camped around her
home as well. He seemed pissed about it. He said he
would just wait until Terrence came out. The demon
told me he tells Terrence what to do and he does it.
He said he would patiently wait because Terrence would
eventually come out. He was leaning against the car
just chilling. The demon then said I should go check
on my son. When I went to go check on my son there was
bobwire around his head and neck and he was struggling
to breath. I tried to take it off but could not. I
woke up in a panic. I instantly went into the bathroom
and got on my knees to pray. I prayed for about two
hours. I checked on my kids and went to go lay back
down beside Terrence. When he woke up I told him the
dream and he told me I was tripping. He left to go
home and I went about my day. That evening my son
started having trouble breathing. I began to pray and
while praying for him the phone rang and it was my
Pastor. She started praying before I could even tell
her what was wrong. God had grace and mercy on my son
and me! He recovered and that night I called Terrence
to tell him to come and get his stuff. The following
day he came and tried to convince me to stay with him
but I knew better. He took his stuff and I had no more
contact with him except for the occasional hi when I
went to his mother's house for prayer. I was sad about
our relationship ending but most of all I was
devastated because I disobeyed God and almost lost my
son. I knew I had messed up and I thought I lost all
hope of God bringing my "Adam" to me.

Sometime later I visited a church and the Pastor stopped preaching on her topic to preach about falling into sexual sin. She had never shared her testimony before and could not understand why all of sudden she needed to tell hers. Little did she know she was preaching to me. A year later my "Adam" came and I thank God for it!

I believe Terrence had the best intentions toward me but it wasn't good enough. I wouldn't suggest a jail relationship to any woman. You give in every area but he can only give you words. The majority of the time they are empty words. He need to come home and learn how to live again and take care of himself before he can be of any help to you. Another reason why I think I got caught up is because of his mother being a preacher. I listened to her tell me how her sons were raised in the church and they knew God. I was going off of her salvation and not his own. Nevertheless, I heard God and I should have obeyed Him!

Be not wise in your own eyes; reverently fear and
worship the Lord and turn [entirely] away from evil.
Proverbs 3:7 AMP

First, let me say that there are a lot of men who have went to jail, done their time and turned their lives around. Chef Jeff and Judge Mathias are two wonderful examples that I know of. There are probablly many more men who made a move just like them and I praise God for it. I know that God is able to do the miraculous! The story below proves my point.

While waiting on my sister to take her to the store. The Lord told me to get out of my car and walk over to a drug dealer standing in the cut in front of my car. I told my children to stay put and not to move. I locked the car doors and headed toward him. I asked him could I share with him what the Lord told me to tell him. He said, "yeah." I told him God said he was going to take him off the streets and use him to minister to other drug dealers to bring them off the streets. As I was talking to him it was as if he and I were the only ones in the cut, even though I could see the other drug dealers watching us. The atmosphere around him and I was powerful. When I finished telling him what the Lord said, I asked him could I hug him and he said, "yeah." When I did I began to speak in my heavenly prayer language. When God finished I told him thank you and walked back to my car. My sister stood there watching, we got in the car and drove off. I told her what happened and she praised God. Everytime he saw my sister after that he asked her was I still praying for him. She would tell him yes, and I was. This went on for several months. By the time a year rolled around he had stopped selling drugs, got a job, and moved his family out of the projects. Praise God for the things He has done! That brother took the word of the Lord and ran with it.

If you are with a man who has been released from jail and he has no plans of changing his life and walking it out, then you need to move on. Do not waste your time! Trust God and wait on Him to bring you your "Adam!"

Chapter 16

PRAYER

Father, I thank you for this opportunity to pray for my "Adam." Lord, you know exactly where he is and what he is doing. You know all about his life. Father, show him the error of his ways that he may repent and turn from his sinful ways. Forgive him of his sins, Lord. Create in him a clean heart and renew a right spirit within him that he may walk upright before you. I ask that you would heal him from his past and deliver him from any sin that has made a stronghold in his life. Father heal his heart from wounds that life may have brought him. Make him a man after your own heart that he may serve only you. Allow your love to fill his heart that he may be able to love me, his family and others unconditionally. Give him wisdom knowledge and understanding that he may lead his family in the fear and admonition of you. And when you are ready let him find me. For your word say, "he that findeth a wife findeth a good thing and obtaineth favor from the Lord." I pray this by faith, in your son Jesus name, Amen!

PART 3

WE

Chapter 17

CAN THERE BE A WE

If you belong to God who you marry is just as important as where you live, where you attend school, or any other major decision you will make in your lifetime. You can not afford to link your life with someone who does not have the same beliefs and goals that you have. To do this will be disasterous and will draw you away from God and His will for your life. Don't just think about yourself when making this decsion. Think about God first because He will be the one you will run to if it doesn't work out. Think about any children you may have now or will have after you are married. How you raise your children will be affected by whom you marry. A young boy asked his grandmother will his mother go to hell because she is married to a Muslim. She told him no and he was very relieved. This young man was raised in the Lord so he has a good understanding of what the Lord requires. Even still he knows something is amiss with this union. So, please do not take this matter lightly.

When I first started dating seriously my mother would want to meet my date. She would ask me questions like, "Where did you get him from"? "What do his parents do for a living"? "Do insanity run in his family"? I felt these line of questions were unneccessary. So, I would not bring my dates to my house. I thought she was being old fashioned but she was using wisdom and pulling from life experiences. Now I realize these type of questions are necessary before you decided to tie the knot.

Before my husband came into my life God showed my pastor at the time that he was a preacher or pastor. We were in prayer and she revealed to me that she could see him walking back and forth praying earnestly to the Lord. A few years later while on the bus a woman that I did not know gave me a prophetic word to hold on because my husband was on the way and that he was a man of God. I never asked God for a word, I just prayed quitely in my heart. Right before my husband showed up I had an encouter that I will never forget. I was in my bedroom sitting at the end of the bed. My children had just fallen asleep and I looked down the hall into the living room to see Satan himself come through the wall. He was headed straight for me. I was shocked, I did not know what to do. When he reached the the living room door I saw an angel come through the door with his arm outstretched. He grabbed satan around his neck and they both went out the other side of the apartment. The next thing I new satan was walking down the hall again by the kitchen and the angel came again with the same force and they went out the other side of the apartment. Satan came one more time and this time he was by the bathroom door. The angel came against him again with the same force and the next thing I knew Jesus was in front of my bedroom door, protecting me with his glory. I just stared in amazement! Once the cost was clear Jesus looked at me and said, "I am leaving Michael here to protect you." I told him, "ok." Jesus left and Michael was standing at my front door guarding it. He looked powerful and fierce. In my brilliance I ask him a question from where I was sitting at, on the bed. I do not remember what it was but he did not answer. I did not take offense because he was on duty and I was glad he was there. I laid down next to my son and went to sleep. A few months later my "Adam" showed up.

I met my husband online and when we agreed to meet
for the first time I did not like what I saw and
neither did he. He was attracted to petite light
complextion women with big breast. I on the other hand
was attracted to dark complexion men with pretty
white teeth, bright eyes and nice feet. Despite our
reservations we continued to see each other and had
planned to spend Thanksgiving together with my
children. A day before Thanksgiving I called him and
told him I did not want him to come over. I told him I
did not think it was going to work out between us. I
knew he was hurt but I did not care. On Thanksgiving
day I was stiring sweet potato filling and watching
the Oprah show. BeBe and CeCe Winans was on singing.
Instantly, I heard the Lord say in a stern voice, "Who
are you to reject what I have blessed?" I apologized
to God, put that bowl down and called him right away
to aologize. He accepted my apology and we made
arrangements to spend Christmas together. During this
time it still mattered to me how my children felt
about him. If they did not like him I would not have
married him despite all that had taken place. When my
children received him along with my two neice's and
spiritual brother. I knew that God was in it for sure.
You cannot get anything past children! This sealed the
deal for me. We were told by the Lord to stay holy and
He would bless us. He also commanded us to pray
everyday together until the marriage ceremony. We did
it without fail. One night we went to a prayer meeting
at my pastors house and a friend of my pastor told us
that he was my husband and to set a date right now.
We looked at each other and he set a date right then
and there. Three months later we were married and to
top it off God in His goodness had a wonderful woman
of God to pull me aside before the wedding to assure
me that he was my husband. My husband and I first
sexual encounter was on our wedding night. We have
been together ever since.

Remember, who you marry covers you and whatever
spirit rule in your husband's life will rule over you
and your household. If it is a religious spirit then
you will experience an outward form of godliness from

him but he will deny the power of the Holy Spirit.
This ruling spirit will invite other spirits to come
in and reign in your home. This spirit will do
everything to stop the power of the Holy Ghost from
moving in your life and in your home.

There was a man named Nabal who was rich but was
mean and surly. His name means fool or foolish. He was
married to a woman named Abigail. She was a beautiful
woman with wisdom. Her name means a father's joy.
David was on the run from King Saul and while in
Carmel David made this request to Nabal.

*"Peace and prosperity to you, your family, and
everything you own! I am told that it is sheep-
shearing time. While your shepherds stayed among us
near Carmel, we never harmed them, and nothing was
ever stolen from them. Ask your own men, and they
will tell you this is true. So would you be kind to
us, since we have come at a time of celebration?
Please share any provisions you might have on hand
with us and with your friend David." David's young
men gave this message to Nabal in David's name, and
they waited for a reply. 1 Samuel 25:6-9 NLT*

Being a foolish man Nabal replied.

*"Who is this fellow David?" Nabal sneered to the young
men. "Who does this son of Jesse think he is? There
are lots of servants these days who run away from
their masters. Should I take my bread and my water
and my meat that I've slaughtered for my shearers and
give it to a band of outlaws who come from who knows
where?" 1 Samuel 25:10-11 NLT*

This pissed David off and he put on his sword along
with four hundred of his men to go and kill Nabal. One
of Nabal's servants heard what David planned to do and
told Abigail what happened. She packed up food and
supplies and went to go meet David and his men before
they reached her home. Abigail humbly greets David and
her words of wisdom appeased his anger. She asked him
to remember her when he comes into his kingdom. He
told her to go home in peace, that he would not kill
her husband.

*When Abigail arrived home, she found that Nabal was
throwing a big party and was celebrating like a king.
He was very drunk, so she didn't tell him anything
about her meeting with David until dawn the next day.
In the morning when Nabal was sober, his wife told him
what had happened. As a result he had a stroke, and he
lay paralyzed on his bed like a stone. About ten days
later, the LORD struck him, and he died. 1 Samuel
25:36-38 NLT*

When David found out Nabal had died he sent for
Abigail.

*When David heard that Nabal was dead, he said, "Praise
the LORD, who has avenged the insult I received from
Nabal and has kept me from doing it myself. Nabal has
received the punishment for his sin." Then David sent
messengers to Abigail to ask her to become his wife. 1
Samuel 25:39 NLT*

Now do you see why it matters to God who you marry?
Abigail did not have a choice in her marriage to Nabal
because in that day marriages where arranged by the
parents. She lived in bondage with this man. You have
a choice and I pray you will choose wisely.

Chapter 18

IS HE MARRIAGE MATERIAL

Here are some key questions a Christian women should ask herself when dating and before marrying. These questions should help you to weed out the counterfiet "Adam".

- Is this man a born again believer?
- Do he confess with his mouth that Jesus is Lord?
- Is he filled with the Holy Ghost with the evidence of speaking in tongues?
- Do he walk in holiness (having a made up mind to live for Christ and obey His word)?

- Do his life reflect the fruit of the spirit(love, patience, joy, peace, kindness, forgiveness)? Please do not confuse a form of godliness with holiness (Read Galatians chapter 5)
- Do he actively seek God in prayer and read his bible daily?
- Do he initiate prayer any other time besides saying grace?

- Do he pray in his heavenly prayer language?
- Do he openly share Christ with you and others?
- Do he initiate conversations about Christ and His word?
- Do he listen and take correction as a son?
- Do he admit when he is wrong?
- Do he genuinely apologize?
- Do he take responsibilty for his actions?
- Do he take care of any children he may have (financially, spiritually, emotionally and physically).
- Do he actively live a sexually pure lifestyle?
- Is he determined to wait until marriage to have sex?
- During a trial, do he seek God first or do he run to you or others when problems arise?
- Is he honest?
- Is he trustworthy?
- Do he call or show up when he say he will?
- Do you have similar likes and goals in common?
- Do he have a job and/or career? Is he financially stable?

I recently spoke to a old friend who I had not heard from in a while. He was still funny and animated as ever but I could tell that drugs had ruled its ugly head in his life. While listening to him share the things that had been going on in his life, he was spitting scripture like Kayne raps. All that word in him and it had not changed his life one bit. I thought about if I was single, new in Christ and heard the word come out of him like a river. I would have been fooled. I would have mistaken religion for a personal relationship with God. I would have looked past the obvious, his drug problem and focused on the

scriptures that was coming out of his mouth. I would
have thought as long as he is a Christian (backslidden
or professing) it would not matter, he would make a
good husband. When I shared my thoughts with a Pastor
who knew him as well she told me she did not care what
anybody thought of this man, if he had the right wife
who would work with him he would be awesome. This is
the same thing I heard from his mother for many years.
She would always blame his wife for his behavior and
never hold him accountable for anything he did wrong.
Ladies, you can not change a man nor make him into the
man you want him to be. Only God can change him, if he
allow it. I beg of you not to overlook the works of
the flesh (drugs, lust, pride, etc) that is
manifesting in a man's life. Thinking your love,
money, looks and sex can change him is the biggest
mistake you will ever make in your life!

Chapter 19

RED FLAGS NOT OT OVERLOOK

- If the Holy Ghost alarm go off in your spirit then take heed. If you feel like something is not right, its not. I beg of you to move on and ask God questions later.

- He is a unbeliver.
- If his conversation revolve around sex or he make sexual advances that make you uncomfortable. He should respect your person at all times.
- He lives a worldly lifestyle; drinking, smoking, cussing, clubing, etc.
- He is not honest or trustworthy
- He is secretive about his life. You have never met his family or friends. He can only see you on certain days or hours.
- He is selfish. All he thinks about is himself.
- Your children don't like him.
- He does not take care of his children (financially, spiritually, emotionally and physically). If he do not take care of his

children what makes you think he will take care of
yours? And if he do take care of your kids and not
his own you are an accessory to his crime of being
a deadbeat father.

- You have to remind him how bless he is to have
  you.

- He do not have a job or cannot keep one.

Chapter 20

FLOW CHART FOR MARRIAGE

   The Lord gave me these charts on the following pages
after talking to a co-worker. She wanted to make some
extra money to pay for her wedding. She was a
psychologist. She was beautiful on the inside and out.
She had a wonderful personality and was a joy to be
around. One day she began to talk to me about her
relationship with her fiancé. She told me he was
selfish. He would rather buy five hundred dollars
shoes and expensive suits instead of putting his money
toward the wedding. She even shared with me how they
went to a restaurant one time and he scolded her
because she was laughing too much. It hurt her
feelings. This was her personality and it made her who
she was. On another occasion while chatting in the
break room she looked at me with alarm and said, "I
shouldn't marry him." I asked why she was marrying him
then. She said because her family is all excited about
her getting married and she has already put out all
this money. So, she felt like she had to continue with
the plans. She shook those thoughts off and said,
"Maybe I am being silly." I knew she was not.

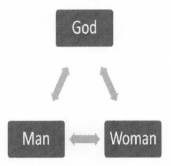

This is how God created the marriage relationship to flow. There has to be a continual flow from each person in order for your marriage to work.

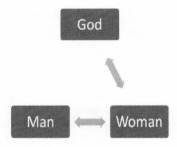

If one person is not connected to God, this interrupts the flow and the marriage is in trouble. You will hear from God but he will not. He will constantly pull from you what he really needs to get from God. This will leave you drained from carrying his load. If he cannot hear from God, how can he lead his family?

Chapter 21

HOW DID I MAKE IT

I made it because of God's grace and mercy, plain and simple! Believe me it was not because of any good works of my own. It was a process. Process is as a series of actions directed toward a particular aim. My aim was a man after God's own heart. I trusted God and believed in the prophets of God for a Holy Ghost filled husband. My actions included me confessing my sins to God. I repented and turned from my sins of fornication and adultery. I forgave until I could feel true forgiveness in my heart. Forgiveness is the key that unlocks closed doors in our lives. If we realized how powerful this commandment is, we would do it quickly and more often. I obeyed God by finalizing my divorce. I had to cut off an ungodly relationship and live holy. I changed my mind set. I gave up my idea(s) of a perfect man. I obeyed God to the best of my ability. When I sinned, I quickly repented and moved on. I prayed without ceasing and I fasted. I read my bible and meditated on scriptures that dealt with my situation. I kept index cards with scriptures on them so that I could pull them out and read them anywhere I was. I was given a wonderful book called "Sending up Timbre" by my pastor at the time, Tonia Brown. She wrote this book of prayers for women who desired a God given mate.

She and Pastor Sarah Stewart watched over my soul and kept me in prayer. These women held my arms up like Aaron and Hur held up the arms of Moses. There were many days filled with tears and some with laughter. I poured out my heart to God all the time. I read books the Holy Spirit directed me to read. I received the love, wisdom, and rebuke of God and the two women who held my arms up and kept me in prayer. I did all these things until my "Adam" came.

Do not worry about how God is going to send you your "Adam." Remember when Elijah thought he was the only prophet left serving God. God gently reminded him that he was not. He told Elijah he had seven thousand more prophets who had not bent their knees to Baal. The same applies to you! God has an "Adam" for you. So, do not fret, just wait on Him. A friend of mine said to me, "It was eight years ago when God sent you your husband." "Times have changed." I told her timing makes no difference to God. Time is an issue for us but not for Him. If God did it for me eight years ago, He will do it for you now! He has no respect of person.

In closing, I pray this book have opened your eyes to any silly behavior you may be exhibiting. I hope the stories in this book stop you from wasting any more time in ungodly relationships. You are worth more than that! I pray you will begin to love yourself enough to move on. I pray that the LORD will bless and protect you, and that he will show you mercy and kindness. May the LORD be good to you and give you peace.

Chapter 22

Prayer

Father, I praise your holy name. I say hallelujah to the Lamb of God. I come before you with a grateful heart. Let your precious blood cover me as I enter into your presence. Lord, I confess that I have not walked upright before you in the area of dating and love. I have let my desires for a mate over rule your will for my life. My fear of being alone and the need to please men and my flesh have cost me dearly. Lord, forgive me for walking in a way that seemed right to me. Forgive me for obeying the dictates of my flesh. Renew my mind in this area that I may obey your word. Give me a clean heart that I may serve only you. My desire is to live holy before you. Sever every soul-tie; deliver me from lust and every unclean spirit that I may be pleasing to you. I present my body this day as a living sacrifice; holy and acceptable to you which is my reasonable service. Let no man deceive me neither let me deceive myself in this matter. Expose all men that would come as wolves in sheep clothing. Help me to stand firm in my convictions and reject every false way. Prepare me for my "Adam" as you did for both Ruth and Esther. Beautify me with your

*holiness and make me into the woman any Father would
be proud to give away, in your son Jesus name, Amen!*

ONE FINAL NOTE:

The stories written in this book are not to shame or embarrass anyone. I love and respect every woman and their stories. I purposely omitted or changed the names to protect all those involved.

I wrote the book because God gave me the title and told me to write it. I fought with Him over a span of four years concerning this book and in the end He won. **He always wins!**

This book is intended to be used as a tool, gauge, guide and/or warning when it comes to how we should live our lives as godly women.

I make no apologies for obeying God and if the stories in this book stop a thousand women, one hundred, ten or even one woman from committing the same sins and making the same mistakes written in this book, then I have successfully done my job!

God Bless,

Theresa Hornes

77200408R00104

Made in the USA
Middletown, DE
19 June 2018